The
Good Taste
Guide
through
Normandy

❋

The
Good Taste
Guide
through
Normandy

⚜

JULIAN WORTHINGTON

foulsham
LONDON • NEW YORK • TORONTO • SYDNEY

foulsham

The Publishing House, Bennetts Close,
Cippenham, Berkshire, SL1 5AP, England

General Disclaimer
While every effort has been made to ensure the accuracy of all the information contained within this book, neither the author nor the publisher can be liable for any errors. In particular, since businesses change from time to time, it is vital that each individual should check all relevant details for themselves.

ISBN 0-572-02219-0

Printed in Great Britain by Edmundsbury Press,
Bury St Edmunds, Suffolk.

Contents

Introducing the guide

Those unfortunate enough never to have experienced the veritable delights of this northern coastal region of France could be forgiven for dismissing Normandy simply as the original home of one William the Conqueror or, more recently, the stage for a dramatic series of landings that hastened the demise of one of the world's greatest tyrants.

Having once set foot on Norman soil, viewed the rich and fertile landscape and tasted the splendours of its produce and cuisine, however, there could surely not be a person alive who would not pass a few mournful reflections on those lost – even wasted – years of ignorance. Waste no more time, take this guide and enjoy.

Although there may be those among us who prefer not to dwell on some of the more dramatic moments of history, it is impossible to ignore the heritage of Normandy itself and the pride and purpose of its people. And nowhere is this more clearly illustrated than in its long-established and world-renowned traditions of good food and good eating.

For this is a land of grazing meadows, fruit orchards, field after field of vegetables and an ever-changing coastline that provides some of the finest shellfish in Europe. No wonder, then, that mouth-watering spreads daily dress even the most modest of tables and that the region is blessed with a multitude of eating establishments all offering their own specialities to whet the appetite of the discerning – and not so discerning – diner.

No meal, of course, is complete without a glass (or two!), although those in search of a local bottle of France's most celebrated beverage will be disappointed. Normandy is not one of France's wine-producing areas. Still, one can always take consolation by sampling its cider, calvados and *pommeau* – a trio of drinks for which the region is justly noted.

Equally famous is the dairy produce and in particular cheese, including one of France's best-known – camembert. And where there is cheese, and butter and cream, naturally there is milk ... and cows. Here the rich pastures guarantee high-quality meat, which the Normans definitely cook to perfection.

One could go on, since the list is seemingly endless. But *The Good Taste Guide through Normandy* is not just about food and drink, fine though these obviously are. It has been specially prepared to provide

1

all those visiting the region with the right kind of information to maximise the inevitable pleasure of their stay – however long or short that might be.

Unlike most general guide books, this one takes you to the very heart of Norman life – the people themselves. It tells you, for example, exactly where to go to meet the oyster farmers and the cheese and cider makers. Here you will be able to relive centuries of tradition, while gaining first-hand knowledge of the work involved in producing the specialities that for many thousands of inhabitants are essential for their very existence.

To help make your journey through Normandy as enjoyable and relaxing as possible, special routes have been set out and information included as to where to stop and eat and where to stay. While these have been carefully selected to give you a 'good taste' of the region, they can – and should, of course – be adapted to suit each traveller.

Those who wish to include more traditional sightseeing have not been forgotten, since the guide also highlights places of historical interest or natural beauty in passing. But it should be stressed here that such information is not intended to be in any way comprehensive. That is not the purpose of this book.

Equally, those looking to buy the cheapest wine or beer from one of the many hypermarkets in the region will be sadly disappointed. *The Good Taste Guide through Normandy* is about quality – not quantity. It is there to help you find interesting souvenirs, keepsakes and presents, so that you can take home and treasure the memories of your holiday.

Whether you are planning just a long weekend or maybe a week or two's holiday, *The Good Taste Guide through Normandy* is full of ideas and advice on making the most of your time in discovering the many local delights and specialities and getting to know the area and its people very much better.

A Taste of Normandy

The infinite variety of special-ities in this region will become all too evident as you travel through the different *départements*. Though many of the products are common to more than one area, there is a local pride – and flavour – which makes each that little bit different as you pass from town to town, village to village.

Without wishing to create any artificial distinctions be-tween the *départements* of Normandy, it is certainly worth highlighting the characteristics of each to help you in your choice of route and destination. For those who have the time, of course, an extensive tour of the whole region will provide the ideal solution.

Incidentally, if you were not already aware of the fact, Normandy is actually divided into two. There is Haute Normandie, which includes the *départements* of Seine-Maritime and Eure and whose capital is Rouen, and Basse Normandie, which is made up of Calvados, Manche and Orne, with Caen as its capital. When you come across this distinc-tion, which some inhabitants of each 'sub-region' will tend to emphasise, then at least you will understand what they are talking about.

The following pages give some background to the region and a sample taste of what you can expect on your travels.

Calvados the *département* is – like its stimulating namesake – at the very heart of Normandy and its history, the area having seen at least two of the most significant moments in Franco-British history over this millenium.

For it was at Caen that William the Conqueror married his distant cousin Princess Mathilda of Flanders, an alliance that gave rise to a couple of extraordinary monuments commissioned to pacify the Church, which disapproved of the union.

The Abbaye-aux-Hommes was begun in 1066 (the year William launched his famous conquest) in Roman style but was completed in the 13th century with a much more Gothic flavour. For her part, Mathilda had the Abbaye-aux-Dames (naturally enough) built between 1060 and 1080. Both architectural curiosities merit a visit to a town that was in the 18th century nicknamed Venise Normande – or Norman Venice – but which structurally fared badly during the Liberation of France in 1944.

The D-Day landings on the beaches of Normandy, which made this turning-point in the Second World War possible, have been suitably commemorated by a grateful nation and a trip along the coast from Carentan to the port of Ouistreham will provide some unforgettable moments.

Monuments and museums are almost too numerous to mention. But the American cemetry at Coleville with row after row of small white crosses – 10,000 in all – is a particularly moving sight. There is also a new and very striking monument as you enter into Bayeux from Caen, where no visit would be complete without a look around the Mémorial Pour La Paix, reflecting the struggle of millions during two world wars to win peace and freedom for the people of Europe.

Turning the clock back nearly a thousand years, you should also make sure you follow all 70 metres of the rich embroidery that relates the events surrounding William the Conqueror's accession to the English throne. The Bayeux Tapestry is one of Normandy's most valuable treasures.

The landscape of Calvados is as varied as anywhere in the region – a perfect blend of coastline, woodland, pastureland and plains. Such a mixed palette of colour offered by its diverse scenery has been the inspiration of many an artist, and nowhere more so than at Honfleur, with its old port surrounded by charming little houses. The works of the 'Honfleur School' are displayed in the Eugène Boudin art museum.

Make sure while you are here to work up a sufficiently healthy appetite to try the local speciality – *teurgoule*. This is a milky rice pudding topped with caramel which is cooked for up to four hours – quite delicious as an end to any meal.

Where there is coastline, of course there is seafood – and Calvados is no exception, boasting several large fishing ports. The most important is Port-en-Bessin, the sixth largest in France in terms of volume fished. Here at the *criée* (the wholesalers' market) there is an almost unlimited variety of fish to be found: sole, plaice, brill, turbot, whiting, conger eel, dogfish, scallops, lobsters, crabs … one could go on. It is possible to visit the market at certain times and you should certainly do so given the chance.

While on the subject of food, mention should be made of two

specialities in particular. The first is the *Andouille de Vire*, whose gastronomic traditions date back to the 18th century. The *andouille* is prepared with a pig's digestive tract, which is washed, blended and smoked for six to eight weeks. It is then soaked, tied up with string and cooked in water for three to four hours.

The real secret of making a good andouille involves two factors: the cleanliness of the offal and the long smoking process. It should have a strong and robust flavour. In fact, you should be able to taste the Calvados soil in the Andouille de Vire.

The second culinary masterpiece – again using offal, but do not be put off by that – is *Tripes à la mode de Caen*. Legend attributes the initial popularity of this dish to our old friend William the Conqueror, who was a great fan of tripe. The original recipe is very precise, requiring five types of beef offal cut into large pieces and boiled until the juice is clear, limpid and not too fatty. Nowadays it is quite likely that a little calvados will find its way into the tripe while it is cooking, just to add a touch more flavour.

Talking of which … you could be forgiven for being slightly baffled by the inclusion of *Trou Normand* in the middle of a long restaurant menu of many courses. This 'Norman Hole' is in fact a small glass of calvados. The idea behind this old tradition is that it helps to digest the first part of the meal and stimulates the appetite for the rest, should you need the excuse! A modern variation comes in the form of an apple sorbet soaked in the local brandy.

Eure

Embracing the lower reaches of the River Seine, which twists and turns its relentless way towards and through the centre of the French capital, the *département* of Eure boasts, among many treasures, a nature lover's haven – Marais-Vernier, tucked into the final loop of the mighty river before it reaches the busy port of Le Havre and opens out into the English Channel.

By skirting the market gardens, with their many varieties of trees and reed beds, you will arrive first at the Manneville Reserve, where Scottish cows – direct descendants of the aurochs – and migratory birds live together and undisturbed among rare flora, lovingly preserved thanks to the efforts of the Parc Naturel Régional de Brotonne.

Just to the south of Marais-Vernier you will find the town of Pont-Audemer, full of charm and surprises. This was formerly a tannery centre. Here you can stroll along the canals – and across them via the numerous small bridges – and explore the many alleyways and cul-de-sacs lined with half-timbered houses. Look out for the superb staircases in carved wood and the remains of the former tan pits. Remember, also, to include in your tour the church, the library and the Canal Museum.

Two of the most impressive châteaux in the area are those of Harcourt and Gaillard, each in their own different way offering a rare treat for the visitor.

Sited to the south-east of Brionne, Château d'Harcourt was built at the end of the 12th century. This enchanting spot is surrounded by lush vegetation, its wall includes no less than eight towers and there is also an arboretum containing more than 200 species of tree.

There is a definite English connection with Château Gaillard, since it was constructed – again in the 12th century – under the orders of Richard Coeur de Lion, King of England and Duke of Normandy. Its commanding site, high up on a cliff overlooking the Seine, provides superb views of the meandering river and the numerous little islands to be found along this stretch of the river.

Manche

Manche is the most westerly of the *départements* of Normandy and boasts the longest coastline. This takes in the Cotentin Peninsula to the north and runs right down to Le Mont-Saint-Michel in the south. On a fine day the Channel Islands are clearly visible and you often have the impression that Jersey is so close that you could actually stretch out and touch it.

It is impossible even to mention Manche without thinking of fish – and most especially oysters. Here, where the sea washes its diverse shores, you will find some of the region's finest oyster beds. Although much of this rich harvest finds its way to the lucrative markets of Paris and other parts of France, you can still buy direct – and not expensively – from the local producers.

The Normandy oysters are principally raised in the Saint-Vaast-la-Hougue and Blainville-Coutainville-Gouville basins and in the western part of the Baie des Veys. This last type is also found in Calvados. Twelve metres from the surface, the oysters filter the purest currents, giving them that inimitable taste of the ocean.

Of course, the sea is home to other shellfish and crustacea, which provide a magnificent plate for those wishing to indulge. These include shrimps, cockles, mussels (which the locals call *caïeux*), *ormeaux* (a shellfish with very fine meat which is collected during high tides), clams (known here as Venus) and carpet shells, which should be eaten with a thick slice of bread and butter (Norman, naturally).

For the real gourmet there are a couple of particular delights not to be missed – the *Demoiselles de Cherbourg* (small lobsters around 300-400g in weight) and the famous *Coquilles Saint-Jacques* (or scallops).

Wherever you go along this part of the Normandy coast, you will come across a whole range of seafood specialities of remarkable freshness and taste. Through their culinary tradition, the Normans have created a thousand and one different ways of preparing such maritime treasures to bring out the very best flavour.

In case you get the impression that the inhabitants of Manche eat nothing but fish, it is worth noting that in the Cotentin region you can also taste a delicious ham, wood-smoked according to traditional methods, and find out about the boning and salting techniques from the craftsmen who specialise in its production.

While on the subject of meat, no visit to the area would be complete without tasting the Mont-Saint-Michel lamb, which is raised on the grassy salt-meadows that the sea covers at high tide. These meadows are enriched with iodine and salt flora, giving the meat an incomparable flavour.

The remarkable village of Le Mont-Saint-Michel, built on a rock in the middle of a vast expanse of sand, has another claim to fame as the home of the omelette, which was originated by one of the Mont's most well-known inhabitants – Mère Poulard. For it was she who had the idea to beat the eggs she accidentally broke and cook them in a pan, thus inventing the world-famous dish.

Another product for which Manche is nationally recognised is the Créances carrot – red, tender and with a deliciously mild flavour. If you are driving south from Cherbourg to Coutances you will pass field after field of this vegetable. And, alternating with it, you will see leeks, which also thrive in the local soil and climate.

Of course, not all the specialities of this *département* are culinary in the sense of being edible. Between Saint-Lô and Avranches, you will come across the town of Villedieu-les-Poêles, renowned among other things for its copper and pewter workshops. Needless to say, the objects produced here include kitchen utensils, much sought after by France's top chefs.

A trip to Villedieu-les-Poêles will also provide you with the chance to visit one of only two bell foundries still in existence in France.

Orne

It is bound to come as quite a surprise for the first-time visitor to know that part of the region has been nicknamed Suisse Normande – or Norman Switzerland. More precisely, this takes in the western woodland area of Orne.

Its rugged landscape of unending hills, totally out of character with the rest of Normandy, is indeed reminiscent of the Basle region of Switzerland. But before you get carried away into packing your skis, the similarities are in fact only visual.

For those who enjoy walking, this is ideal hiking countryside. One of the most spectacular routes begins at Putanges-Pont-Ecrepin, to the south of Falaise,

and runs alongside the Orne river itself, past the lake and dam of Rabodanges and through the gorges of Saint-Aubert, finishing up at Pont-d'Ouilly.

This tour will provide everyone with a suitable taster. Of course, there are many other routes you can discover for yourselves to relish all the stunning scenery in this region.

It is interesting to note that this part of Normandy was the cradle of dairy farming and gave birth to what are now some of the region's most famous and lucrative industries – notably the production of cheese, butter and chocolate.

It is the Orne, in fact, which boasts the home of Normandy's most famous cheese – Camembert – named after its birthplace, a small village to the south-west of Vimoutiers.

History records that it was one Marie Harel who in 1791 invented what has arguably become one of France's most well-known exports. Following the advice of an old priest, who had fled from his home town of Brie during the French Revolution, she began making the cheese which has since become a veritable symbol of the region.

An interesting footnote here is that it was nearly a hundred years later – 1890 to be precise – that a certain Monsieur Ridel created the famous round wooden box in which Camembert is still marketed today.

It is impossible to talk about the *département* of Orne without mentioning its horses, since it is here that some of the finest stallions in France are bred. A veritable jewel in the equine crown is the Haras du Pin National Stud to the east of Argentan.

Founded in 1665 by a Monsieur Colbert and often referred to as the 'horse's Versailles', this establishment houses eight different breeds of stallion which are distributed each spring through the district's 23 stud farms to produce some of the finest bred horses in Europe. A free guided tour includes visits to the magnificent stables and saddle rooms and round the terraces and gardens designed by Le Nôtre.

This area has other treasures not to be missed, such as the splendid historical homes in Médavy, Carrouges and Flers and religious monuments such as the cathedral at Sées. To complete the visit, a trip to Alençon to admire the fine collection of lace and the various techniques used, dating back to the 16th century, will provide its own reward.

Seine-Maritime

Presenting an almost mirror image of the chalky white cliffs of Sussex just the other side of The Channel, the Alabaster Coast – with its famous Aiguille d'Etretat – is among the most spectacular of all Normandy's extensive shoreline.

Dramatically carved by thousands of years of natural erosion, the breathtaking rugged cliffs that stretch 75 miles from Le Havre to Le Tréport contrast vividly with the otherwise green and fertile landscape of the rest of the *département* of Seine-Maritime.

Here as much as anywhere else in the region the sea, and more particularly the ports have had a vital role to play in the lives of the inhabitants. Le Havre not only welcomes cross-Channel visitors from Britain but also boasts being the second largest port in France. Dieppe offers an alternative gateway for travellers, as well as being an important fishing harbour.

There is historically quite an oriental connection with this part of Normandy. Going back as far as Renaissance times, ivory was imported into and carved at Dieppe. Examples of these sculptures can be seen in the Château Museum. And it is via Dieppe that the spices pass on their way to Fécamp to help make the world-famous Benedictine liqueur.

Benedictine was originally a healing elixir concocted by a monk of that order in 1510. Thanks to the efforts of Alexandre Legrand, a dynamic entrepreneur of Fécamp, it was marketed as a liqueur from around 1860. The secret recipe contains no less than 27 herbs and spices, including pine buds, genepi, cinnamon, aloe, vanilla and juniper berries.

Incidentally, the distillery is part of a sumptuous religious palace dating from the 15th and 16th centuries, which also includes an art gallery.

There is, happily, no secret about the fine local fish, which you can enjoy almost everywhere. The inhabitants of this stretch of coastline have certainly mastered the art of taste and presentation and you should not miss the chance of trying the Fécamp mackerel, herring *à la Havraise* or whiting *à la Dieppoise*.

Travelling inland and to the south-east of Dieppe, you will arrive at Neufchâtel-en-Bray, a town particularly notable as the home of a suitably strong but delicious cheese – incidentally the oldest in Normandy. It comes in various shapes and sizes, but is especially well-known for its heart-shape.

From both an historical and architectural point of view, Rouen must feature on every itinerary. The very heart of this fine city of a hundred belfries is lined with pretty Norman houses and you should take time to stroll around its narrow streets, past the magnificent cathedral and into the Place du Vieux-Marché, where the unfortunate Joan of Arc met her fate at the stake in 1431.

Having also taken in the Beffroi and the Gros Horloge (large clock), you will certainly have worked up the appetite to enjoy two of the city's culinary specialities – *Canard à la Rouennaise* and *Sucre de Pomme*.

From Rouen, take the especially interesting drive out to Le Havre – Les Routes du Val-de-Seine et des Abbayes. The road, much of which follows the picturesque windings of the river, carries you past the famous abbeys of Saint-Ouen, Saint-Georges-de-Boscherville, Jumièges, Saint-Wandrille and Montivilliers, as well as a collection of castles and museums.

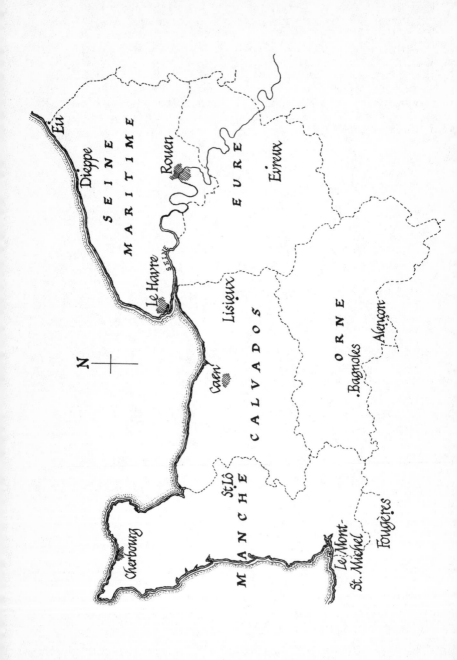

The Flavour of Normandy

You only have to glance at the rich meadows on which Norman cows graze to realise that you are in a region rich in dairy produce, whether it be milk, butter, cream or cheese – all of which have justly gained a reputation for quality and taste.

So seriously is production taken that rigorous standards have been set and special controls imposed. So, as with wine, you will find some products carrying the proud 'Appellation d'Origine Contrôlée' mark. Not only does this protect the items concerned but it also bears proof of their Norman origin and traditional methods of production.

Take for example the crème fraîche bearing the stamp 'AOC d'Isigny', or the four most celebrated cheeses of Normandy – Camembert, Neufchâtel, Pont-l'Evêque and Livarot.

A MILLENIUM OF CHEESE

There is a proud and lasting tradition of cheese-making in Normandy that dates back to at least 1035. Records award the title of the region's oldest cheese to Neufchâtel.

Produced over a 30 kilometre radius around the town of the same name, this cheese is made from cow's milk mixed with rennet. Smooth and creamy, yet firm, it can come in six different shapes, the most distinctive being in the form of a heart. It has had AOC recognition since 1969.

Manufactured by monks under the name of Angelot in the early 12th century, it was not until around 1720 that Pont-l'Evêque won more than local acclaim. Granted an AOC in 1976, this is a warm cheese with an especially fine flavour. Its fruity refined taste will prove an unforgettable treat for the most delicate of palates.

First made in the small town in the Vallée d'Auge bearing its name, Livarot certainly dates from at least 1690. In 1708 it was highly praised by the brother of the writer Pierre Corneille, who was won over by its original taste and high nutritional value. Production has grown sharply since the 19th century and since 1975 it has enjoyed AOC protection.

The most famous of Normandy – and, arguably, French – cheeses is the ladle-moulded Camembert made from raw milk. Strict manufacturing controls guarantee the absolute quality of this cheese, which was awarded its AOC in 1983.

Take the beef and veal that carry the 'Label Régional Normandie', which provides a guarantee that the cattle have been reared on rich local pastures and the calves fed with natural whole milk. Take the naturally raised farm pigs that bear the 'Label Rouge' and provide the excellent charcuterie, pâtés, ham as well as the renowned *Andouille de Vire*, a type of chitterling sausage.

You can add to this impressive list the firm-fleshed poultry and, in particular, the ducks and geese from which the delicious Norman foie gras comes, not forgetting the lambs reared on the salt meadows of Mont-St-Michel Bay, which give the meat a very special flavour. And, of course, there is the fish and crustacea – perfect whether eaten fresh or smoked or in the delicious terrines or marinades.

The local beverages come under the same strict controls – like the cider, which is now to be given official AOC status, something which calvados already enjoys along with only two other French brandies, cognac and armagnac. The other local drink in the 'apple trio' is the *pommeau de Normandie*, which also preserves its reputation through the system of AOC recognition.

A la carte

However good the ingredients, it is in the preparation and use that their true quality and value are manifested. This has certainly not been lost on the people of Normandy, whose tradition in the culinary arts is legendary. Here, every meal offers the opportunity to exercise the gastronomic skills that have been passed down through generations.

There are several ingredients that have become an integral part of Norman gastronomy. Crème fraîche, for example, can be added to just about any dish on the menu. It is also customary to add a few drops of calvados, pommeau or the bubbly pure fruit juice cider, all of which help create a unique and festive flavour to both savoury and sweet dishes.

Naturally the exact type of cooking varies, depending on which part of the region you find yourself in. While the ingredients tend to be the same, they are blended in different ways. The four principal styles are Caux, Dieppe, Rouen and Vallée d'Auge.

Caux-style cuisine
You will recognise this by such appetising dishes as 'rabbit marinated in white wine' and 'sole braised in cider'.

Dieppe-style cuisine
Here there is a definite seafood bias – such as fish cooked in white wine, garnished with mussels and shrimps, and served with a white wine and mushroom sauce.

Rouen-style cuisine
This is particularly well-known for its delicious duck dishes.

Vallée d'Auge-style cuisine
One of the great classics is chicken browned in butter, singed in calvados and served with crème fraîche.

The signed routes

One of the very simplest ways of discovering and sampling those specialities that are at the heart of Norman gastronomy is to follow the officially signed routes which will take you to the birthplaces of the products themselves. Naturally you should feel free to stop where you like and make any detours you want – particularly to some of the many interesting cultural and historic sites in each area. Certainly this will ensure that your trip is not completely taken up with eating and drinking!

The main signed routes include:

The Cider Route

This short circuit takes in the picturesque villages of Cambremer, Beuvron-en-Auge, Bonnebosq and Beaufour-Druval, which you can reach via the N13 between Lisieux and Caen or from the N175 south of Dozulé.

Following the pretty hedge-lined roads, here and there you will see some very fine houses, little churches and many fertile orchards, all of which encapsulate the charm of the Pays d'Auge. You will also pass farms with the special 'Cru de Cambremer' sign and are more than welcome to visit their cellars, where you can still see the old presses whose heavy wood and granite grinders are even today used to make cider.

Your reward will be to taste some of the very best cider and calvados in the region.

The Cheese Route

This marked circuit centres round the junction of the D4 and D579 south of Lisieux, between Saint-Pierre-sur-Dives and Orbec, and will enable you to discover a part of the Pays d'Auge known for its rich milk and half-timbered red houses decorated with fragments of pink tile.

There is no better place to taste camembert than from the village of the same name, where it originated, just to the south-west of Vimoutiers – or, for that matter, the variety of cheeses that come from Livarot.

Saint-Pierre-sur-Dives is home to the Musée des Techniques Fromagères – the 'Cheese Museum' – where you can find out about the history of the different cheeses of the region and all the various manufacturing processes.

The Neufchâtel Cheese Route

This tour is based round and to the south of Neufchâtel-en-Bray, which you can reach via the D1 from Dieppe. By visiting the dairies, you can taste for yourself the subtleties of this interesting cheese, which comes in a variety of forms – briquette, square, *bonde* (cylindrical), double *bonde*, heart and large heart.

You should take advantage of this tour to see some of the architectural jewels of the area, such as the Renaissance Château Mesnières-en-Bray and the 13th century church at Bully, along with many other local sites. Admire, too, the splendid view at Sainte-Geneviève-en-Bray.

The Gourmet Route

This fascinating tour, which begins at La Haye-du-Puits south of Cherbourg and to the west of Carentan, will take you through the very heart of Manche and enable you to see, taste and buy the most interesting of this area's specialities at the very places where they are made.

The selection of delights includes biscuits, wood-smoked ham, ladle-moulded camembert made from raw milk, fresh dairy products, apple confectionery, fruits and andouille, as well as artistic and culinary earthenware and copper pots and ornaments.

It is no coincidence that the tours suggested in this guide (see '*In Search of the Specialities of Normandy*') include the areas covered above. The obvious advice is 'to follow your nose' and use the information and directions as they suit you. The possible charm of making detours is that they offer a much wider choice and cover a much larger section of this beautiful region. And, of course, if you want to escape your fellow tourists …

The Spirit of Normandy

Some of Normandy's many delicious products come from the apple orchards for which the region is, of course, renowned. And three in particular are most regularly to be tasted by the glass! However, do not be surprised if they also enrich the occasional dish since the Normans are not the sort of people to look far for an excuse to add something extra to their cuisine and make even the most appetising food a little more so!

We are talking, of course, of calvados (which, although bearing the name of one of the region's *départements*, is produced throughout the area), cider (of which there are two kinds – still and sparkling, called *bouché*) and *pommeau* (basically a blend of calvados and cider). All three, it should be said, must be treated with respect. And for the first-time tasters, particular care should be taken with calvados – sometimes veritable 'fire water' when produced *à la ferme*.

A little tip here for the wary. If you are not sure, dip a sugar lump in the calvados and try that first. And don't worry. The Normans do it too!

The other regional drink is *poiré* – a perry made from pears rather than apples. This is particularly to be found in the wooded area around and to the north of Domfront.

The art of making calvados

The making of calvados is an art that the Normans have mastered over centuries of production with their usual flare for the palate. It is prepared in three stages – distillation, ageing and blending.

Distillation
This follows the normal principles, whereby cider is heated to enable the alcohol contained in it to evaporate. Through the subsequent phase of condensation, calvados is obtained.

Ageing
In its 'raw' form in the still, the calvados contains between 68° and 72° of alcohol. By leaving it to age in oak casks, this level is reduced to 40-45°. This ageing process also enhances that distinctive aroma and enables the calvados to change colour – from gold to deep amber.

Blending
The final stage involves blending some 'brandies' of different ages, harvests and soils in order to combine the complementary qualities of each. Following this, the calvados can receive one of two quality control marks depending on where it was produced – Appellation Contrôlée Calvados or Appellation Contrôlée Calvados du Pays d'Auge (where there is a double distillation).

You should bear in mind, however, that not all calvados producers religiously follow the second and third stages, but the 'decontrolled' result can be very acceptable to the more robust palate. Equally, as with other spirits, age will determine the price!

The holy liqueur

There is, of course, another celebrated drink in Normandy – the rich liqueur that comes from the cellars of the Benedictine Palace in Fécamp. Although the exact recipe is a secret well guarded by the monks, its production is there for all to see.

In the Plant Room the basic ingredients – no fewer than 27 different herbs and spices – are carefully nurtured before entering the distillation process. They and the alcohol are converted in copper stills and the precious spirit is then left to age in oak vats.

The Craft of Normandy

Although the specialities of Normandy concentrate mainly on the palate, there are other products to draw the attention of visitors and provide ideal presents and souvenirs of a memorable holiday.

Local crafts are very much a part of this region's heritage and the traditional skills involved in producing a range of different articles date back over many years – even centuries. As always, you can expect a friendly welcome and time spared to discuss and demonstrate all the age-old methods of production.

The following represent a selection of the region's best-known craftsmanship.

Basketwork

Nowhere will you find a better example of this craft than in the village of Remilly-sur-Lozon, situated between Saint-Lô and Périers in the Manche *département*. Here the local craftsmen have been producing wicker baskets for as long as anyone can remember. Not surprisingly, their principal use has been for the local products, such as fruit and bread, although the range extends far beyond these.

Copperware

Without question, the copper and pewter centre of Normandy is to be found at Villedieu-les-Poêles, in the southern part of the Manche *département*. Here they have been 'hammering' metal for more than 300 years and so there are plenty of treasures awaiting today's visitor. You may well discover a Normandy milk can, ewer or old-fashioned vase for sale among a wide range of items. The celebrated bell foundry may not provide the ideal gift, but it is worth a visit all the same.

Lace

Three towns stand out as the centres of what was once a thriving industry, whose products still retain all of their original charm and delicate workmanship. To the north, in the *département* of Calvados, there is Bayeux. Here the art is very much alive and, apart from admiring the displays of lace, you can buy a range of items including handkerchiefs, table mats and cloths. The same is true of Alençon in the Orne *département*, whose rivalry with neighbouring Argentan was legendary. Now the latter simply displays its heritage, the best examples to be seen in the Benedictine abbey there.

Pottery

Historically the most important centre in Normandy for pottery is to be found at Noron-la-Poterie in Calvados, to the south-west of Bayeux, where the manufacture of salt-glaze ware goes back to the 11th century. This speciality is renowned throughout France. Its unique character is due to the quality of the clay, which is fired continuously until vitrified. Originally this process, carried out in a wood-burning kiln, took up to four days. Now it can be done in less than 24 hours. Salt-glazing, which is put on after the firing, gives the pottery a distinctive metallic lustre. You will find many traditional Norman items made here, including the Saint-Gorgon cider pitcher, the *guichon* (a small soup bowl), the *bobin* (a little milk jug) and the *machon* (a pot in which meat, fish, vegetables and eggs are salted down).

If you want to see traditional wood-firing, you should make a visit to Valognes in Manche, which still boasts an original workshop. Among the interesting items made here, you will find the *gohan*, a large receptacle used for taking soup out to the workers in the fields. Ironically, its origins are English.

Weaving

If you are seeking fine furnishing materials, there are several excellent workshops at Périers-sur-le-Dan, to the north of Caen in Calvados. Other original quality items include scarves and ties.

Wrought iron

Naturally enough, there is a long-standing tradition in Normandy for this craft dating back over many centuries. One element that continues to this day is the ornamental fittings for furniture, such as elaborate locks and hinges. You can buy a range of items, rustic as well as modern, from one of the workshops still operating. The best area to head for is Orne and more particularly Alençon and Val-frambert (just to the north) or Chanu and Tinchebray (both to the west of Flers).

LOOK OUT FOR CURIOSITIES

In your travels around Normandy, you are likely to come across some curious items of furniture made from original 'tools of the trade', such as cider presses, equipment used for making calvados and even old salt barrels. Great skill on the part of local craftsmen and women has transformed such relatively mundane items into attractive pieces. These make perfect souvenirs – if you have the room to carry them home!

In Search of the Specialities of Normandy

In addition to the 'official' tourist routes, which you will find marked, we have planned a series of tours in which you will be able to discover the best that the region has to offer. A range of these has been designed to ensure that you can make the most of your visit to Normandy – depending, of course, on what interests you most and the time you have available.

The various towns and villages mentioned are there as central points, around which the group of places worth visiting are situated. They should not, therefore, be considered as necessarily the most important locations but more as practical centres from which you will be able to explore each particular area – essentially to see, taste and purchase the different specialities, but also to enjoy the many interesting sights that Normandy has to offer.

While the different sections of each route have been illustrated to help you on your way, a detailed map of the region will not only ensure you avoid a wrong turn but will also enable you to deviate from the route should you wish. For this purpose, the most practical and useful is the Michelin map of Normandy – No 231.

Depending on the time you have available and your own preferences, of course, you may adapt the recommended routes as you wish.

Although the information provided has been specially selected to help maximise your pleasure and enjoyment, it is by no means exhaustive. You are bound to make your own discoveries en route – and we would be pleased to hear about these.

Visitors are, of course, welcome in all the places mentioned. However, there may be restrictions as to hours or days and certainly large groups should always make a call to check first. Where possible, therefore, telephone numbers have been given and it is wise to make a quick call in advance of any visit.

When out shopping, try to remember that the French take lunch seriously. That means most places will be closed between midday and at least 2pm – sometimes after! But generally they open earlier and close later than in the UK. Some will be open on Sundays – and you may well find the very best markets then. Monday is the most common day for closing.

Bear in mind, too, that it is sensible to book your meal at any restaurant to save disappointment – and this is essential where the need to book is indicated, since the food will be specially prepared for you. It is also advisable since many establishments close on at least one day – and sometimes two – a week. Sunday evening and Monday are probably the most popular. But the 'days off' can and do vary. Generally speaking, however, most places will stay open during the 'season' – that is the summer months.

Apart from the restaurants listed, many – although not all – of the hotels also provide very good meals and you should bear them in mind not just when looking for somewhere to stay the night. While our selection has been made on quality and convenience, the prices cover the complete range – from the inexpensive to the luxurious! If budget is a consideration, then please check first on the likely cost of your meal or your room.

Bonne route!

HOW TO FOLLOW THE GUIDE

Each tour contains a suggested route and a selection of 'centres' within and around which you will find local specialities. Specific information has been listed under individual headings, after a general description of the town or village centre where there are points of interest.

YOUR ROUTE ...
This is simply to help you organise your tour. Doubtless you will want to deviate from this basic framework, particularly where you come across a suitable distraction. And you will need to do so to find many of the places and people listed.

WHAT TO SEE ...
Highlights of the most interesting sights – such as museums, castles, churches and beauty spots – to enhance your visit.

WHAT TO LOOK OUT FOR ...
Particular specialities of the area – though not necessarily all! You may well find others.

WHERE TO GO FOR ...
Names, addresses and phone numbers of the people who make and sell the specialities. These range from shops to farms and factories, where visitors are welcome to look – and hopefully buy!

WHERE TO EAT ...
Inevitably just a selection of restaurants where you can taste some of the region's gastronomic delights.

WHERE TO STAY ...
A selection of hotels – of all types – to help you plan your stay. Hotels listed in the larger towns have been graded to assist selection – L (luxury), M (moderate) and B (budget). Some also have excellent restaurants, although in principle you are not obliged to eat just because you are sleeping there.

Pays de Bray

This tour, which begins at Dieppe, takes you through the Pays de Bray, whose landscape is one of undulating hills, meandering rivers and rich green pastureland, in strict contrast to the wide open spaces of the Pays de Caux. The main produce comes from dairy farming, but you will also find fruit, some cider and, of course, Neufchâtel cheese. Continuing south, you pass through the magnificent beech forest of Lyons before arriving by the Seine. From there you continue on to Rouen, whose city centre is a veritable jewel rich in heritage – before returning northwards to Dieppe.

YOUR ROUTE ...

D925 from Dieppe to Eu.

D1314 to Neufchâtel-en-Bray.

N28 (old road) then D929 to Saint-Saëns.

D38 then D41 to Buchy.

D919 to Forges-les-Eaux.

D921 to Argueil, La Feuillie & Lyons-la-Forêt (D321).

D2 then D1 to Les Andelys.

D313 then D316 to Gaillon.

N15 then N155 to Louviers.

D313 to Elbeuf.

D7 then N15 to Rouen.

N27 to Tôtes & Bacqueville (D149).

D127 to Gueures, Saint-Denis-d'Aclon & Quiberville.

D75 to Dieppe.

See map overleaf.

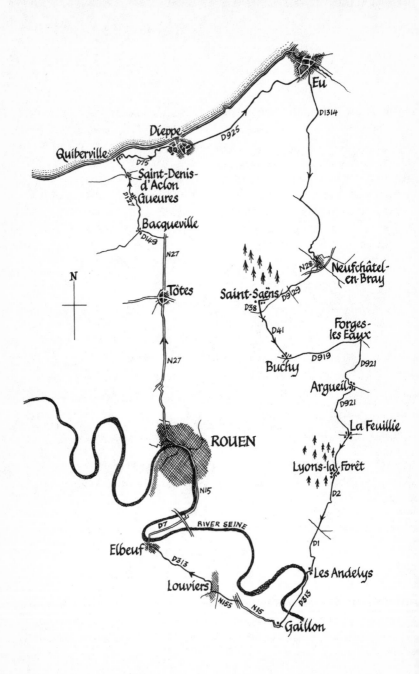

Those who just use this fascinating port as a stepping-off point for more southerly destinations will almost certainly have missed out on the life and charm Dieppe has to offer. From the quayside restaurants and cafés to the narrow streets and alleys of the old town, full of interesting shops and stalls, there is a pleasant surprise round almost every corner. Sadly the ferry from Newhaven no longer docks alongside, since this added to the intimacy of the welcome awaiting the cross-Channel visitor.

The town comes to life early, with the arrival of the fishing fleet. The subsequent market bustles with activity as the catch – mainly of bass, brill, turbot, scallop and sole – is unloaded. But the port is also important for the import of fruit from such faraway places as Morocco, the Cameroon and the Ivory Coast.

The centre is dominated by the impressive Eglise Saint-Jacques, which dates back to the 13th century, and the little streets that feed off it are well worth a stroll round. Try and catch one of the street markets – in Place Nationale and Grande Rue – on Tuesdays, Thursdays and Saturdays. At the far end of the long promenade towers the mainly 15th century Château, which now houses the Municipal Museum. Here you will find an inspiring collection of ivories.

WHAT TO SEE...

Eglise Saint-Jacques, the castle and museum and the Port de Pêche. To the south-east of the town you will find the ruin of the feudal castle at Arques-la-Bataille, perched high on a rock where the Varenne and Béthune rivers meet. Nearby is the village of Martin-Eglise, renowned for its trout fishing. Directly south of Dieppe is Miromesnil Château, which boasts a magnificent Louis XIII facade. It was also the birthplace of the famous French writer Guy de Maupassant. Along the coast, heading west, a view not to be missed is at Phare d'Ailly – a lighthouse from which you can see the Caux cliffs stretching away into the distance.

WHAT TO LOOK OUT FOR...

Crustacea and seafood, especially scallops and sole, and *La Marmite Dieppoise*, a type of fish stew made with angler-fish, turbot, sole, langoustines, scallops and local mussels. Also cider.

WHERE TO GO FOR...

CIDER
Cidrerie et Vergers du Duché de Longueville, Anneville-sur-Scie, nr Dieppe. Tel: 35.04.63.70.

CHEESE
L'Epicier Olivier, 18 rue Saint-Jacques, Dieppe. Tel: 35.84.22.55.

GENERAL GIFTS
Drouin, 105 Grande Rue, Dieppe. Tel: 35.82.57.39.

CONFECTIONERY
Ratel, Grande Rue, Dieppe.

OYSTERS
Goubert, Rue du 19 Août, Pourville-sur-Mer, nr Dieppe. Tel: 35.84.36.20.

TROUT
Pisciculture de la Source, Rue des Basses-Terres, Saint-Aubin-sur-Scie, nr Dieppe. Tel: 35.85.42.88.

HONEY
Marc Fourneaux, Rue de la Côte-Bailly, Saint-Nicholas-d'Aliermont, nr Dieppe. Tel: 35.85.83.86.

Marcel Robart, Chemin d'Hocquelus, Sauchay-le-Bas, nr Dieppe. Tel: 35.85.74.30.

WHERE TO EAT ...

Le Celtic, 95 quai Henri IV, Dieppe. Tel: 35.84.58.50.

Le Clos Sainte-Catherine, 22-24 rue de l'Epée, Dieppe. Tel: 35.84.57.05.

Les Tourelles, 43 rue du Commandant-Fayolle, Dieppe. Tel: 35.84.15.88.

Les Ecamias, 129 quai Henri IV, Dieppe. Tel: 35.84.67.67.

Les P'tits Bateaux, 23 quai Henri IV, Dieppe. Tel: 35.06.14.74.

Restaurant du Port, 99 quai Henri IV, Dieppe. Tel: 35.84.36.64.

Le Galion, 83 quai Henri IV, Dieppe. Tel: 35.82.71.87.

L'Armorique, 17 quai Henri IV, Dieppe. Tel: 35.84.28.14.

A La Marmite Dieppoise, 8 rue Saint-Jean, Dieppe. Tel: 35.84.24.26.

La Musardière, 61 quai Henri IV, Dieppe. Tel: 35.82.94.14.

C Corruble, Hameau de Patteville, Sauqueville, nr Dieppe. Must book. Tel: 35.85.42.16.

WHERE TO STAY ...

A selection of hotels, of all types, to help you plan your stay. Hotels listed in the larger towns have been graded to assist selection – L (luxury), M (moderate) and B (budget). Some also have excellent restaurants, although in principle you are not obliged to eat just because you are sleeping there.

WHERE TO STAY ...

Hôtel La Présidence (L), Boulevard de Verdun, Dieppe. Tel: 35.84.31.31.

Hôtel de l'Univers (L), 10 boulevard de Verdun, Dieppe. Tel: 35.84.12.55.

Hôtel Aguado (L), 30 boulevard de Verdun, Dieppe. Tel: 35.84.27.00.

Le Grand Hôtel (L), 3 boulevard de Verdun, Dieppe. Tel: 35.82.33.60.

Hôtel Windsor (M), 18 boulevard de Verdun, Dieppe. Tel: 35.84.15.23.

Hôtel Les Arcades (M), 1-3 arcades de la Bourse, Dieppe. Tel: 35.84.14.12.

Hôtel Ibis (M), Le Val Druel, Dieppe. Tel: 35.82.65.30.

Hôtel Epsom (M), 11 boulevard de Verdun, Dieppe. Tel: 35.84.10.18.

Hôtel Arcade (M), 6 rue Claude-Groulard, Dieppe. Tel: 35.84.01.84.

Hôtel de la Plage (M), 20 boulevard de Verdun, Dieppe. Tel: 35.84.18.28.

Hôtel Select (M), 1 rue Toustain, Dieppe. Tel: 35.84.14.66.

Hôtel au Grand Duquesne (B), 15 place Saint-Jacques, Dieppe. Tel: 35.84.21.51.

Hôtel Pontoise (B), 10 rue Thiers, Dieppe. Tel: 35.84.14.57.

Tourist Hôtel (B), 16 rue de la Halle-au-Blé, Dieppe. Tel: 35.06.10.10.

L'Eolienne (M), 20 rue de la Croix-de-Pierre, Rouxmesnil-Bouteilles, nr Dieppe. Tel: 35.82.19.50.

Hôtel des Sapins (M), D75, Hameau de Blanc-Mesnil, Sainte-Marguerite-sur-Mer, nr Dieppe. Tel: 35.85.11.45.

La Coquille Fleurie (B), Saint-Aubin-sur-Scie, nr Dieppe. Tel: 35.85.40.22.

This little town just inland from Le Tréport is best known for its collegiate church – Notre-Dame et Saint-Laurent – which dates back to the 11th century. The crypt in particular is worth visiting. The château, which was rebuilt in the late 16th century on the site of a much earlier one, is now the town hall and houses the elegant Musée Louis-Philippe. The park includes a 400-year-old beech tree (Le Guisard). Le Tréport itself has a pleasant fishing harbour and it is worth climbing the 378 steps to take in the view from Calvaire des Terrasses.

WHERE TO GO FOR ...

DAIRY PRODUCE
F Dagicourt, Litteville, Touffreville-sur-Eu, nr Eu. Tel: 35.86.70.92.

Jean-Paul & Nicole Lannel, Melincamp, Saint-Martin-le-Gaillard, nr Eu. Tel: 35.83.51.44.

WHERE TO EAT ...

Le Homard Bleu, 45 quai François 1er, Le Tréport, nr Eu. Tel: 35.86.15.89.

WHERE TO EAT & STAY ...

La Vieille Ferme, 23 rue de la Mer, Mesnil-Val-Plage, nr Eu. Tel: 35.86.72.18.

Le Pavillon de Joinville, Route du Tréport, Eu. Tel: 35.86.24.03.

Neufchâtel-en-Bray

This town, in the heart of the Bray region, is best known for its cheese, for which there is now an *appelation d'origine*. It comes in various shapes and sizes and has a distinctive flavour, particularly when 'ripe'. Among the features in the church are eight windows depicting local saints. The town museum (Musée Mathon-Durand) shows the local traditions and crafts, particularly wrought iron, and includes a cider mill and press.

WHAT TO SEE ...

To the north-west, the magnificent Renaissance castle at Mesnières-en-Bray and the church at Bures-en-Bray, dating from the 12th century.

WHAT TO LOOK OUT FOR ...

Neufchâtel cheese in six different shapes, the smallest weighing 100 grammes and the biggest – the large heart – 600 grammes. Also calvados.

WHERE TO GO FOR ...

CHEESE
Fromagerie L'Hernault, Rue des Abreuvoirs, Neufchâtel-en-Bray.

Léon Boillet, Centre de Massy, Neufchâtel-en-Bray. Tel: 35.93.16.18.

Alex Brianchon, Nesle Hodeng, Neufchâtel-en-Bray. Tel: 35.93.08.68.

Philippe Monnier, Route de Gaillefontaine, Neufchâtel-en-Bray. Tel: 35.94.40.42.

CALVADOS
Gérard Ancel, Ferme des Hattingues, Mortemer, nr Neufchâtel-en-Bray. Tel: 35.94.21.92.

TROUT
Michel Kot, Vatierville, Neufchâtel-en-Bray. Tel: 35.93.11.04.

FRUIT & JAM
Jeanine Levasseur, Ferme Fruitière du Haut-Pas, Bully, nr Neufchâtel-en-Bray. Tel: 35.93.07.13.

WHERE TO EAT & STAY ...

Hostellerie du Grand Cerf, 9 grande rue Fausse-Porte, Neufchâtel-en-Bray. Tel: 35.93.00.02.

Hôtel du Lion d'Or, 17-19 place Notre-Dame, Neufchâtel-en-Bray. Tel: 35.94.77.94.

Saint-Saëns

This small attractive town nestles on the southern edge of the Forêt d'Eawy, one of the finest examples of beech woodland in the whole of Normandy.

WHERE TO GO FOR ...

GOAT'S CHEESE
M-F & G Bazin, Elevage du Val de Bures, Bellencombre, nr Saint-Saëns. Tel: 35.93.90.15.

ANGORA WOOL
Albert Lecoq, Ferme de l'Angora, Beaumont-le-Hareng, nr Saint-Saëns. Tel: 35.33.35.54.

Buchy

WHERE TO GO FOR ...

CIDER
Olivier Laine, Saint-Aignan-sur-Ry, nr Buchy. Tel:35.34.02.36.

FOIE GRAS
Dominique & Marie-Françoise Leblond, Yquebeuf, nr Buchy. Also restaurant – must book. Tel: 35.34.21.74.

HONEY
Gosse-Chivot, 280 rue des Chataigniers, Catenay, nr Buchy. Tel: 35.34.02.40.

This spa town represents a rather grandiose curiosity in an otherwise highly agricultural and wooded environment. Louis XIII and Cardinal Richelieu 'took the waters' here. There is a grotto in the park and a couple of imposing facades – one of an old convent and the other of a royal hunting lodge.

WHERE TO GO FOR...

CHEESE
Patricia Dubois, Route de Neufchâtel-en-Bray, Sommery, nr Forges-les-Eaux. Tel: 35.93.35.56.

Francis Ouin, Sainte-Geneviève-en-Bray, nr Forges-les-Eaux. Tel: 35.90.45.72.

DAIRY PRODUCE
Maurice & Marie-José Defromerie, Ferme de la Chapelle, La Ferté-Saint-Samson, nr Forges-les-Eaux. Tel: 35.90.72.07.

SNAILS
Christophe Lamy, Route de Beaubec, Sommery, nr Forges-les-Eaux. Tel: 35.90.19.41.

This picturesque village with its half-timbered houses lies in the heart of what was once a vast woodland much favoured by the dukes of Normandy for hunting. Les Halles (the covered market) and the 12th century church are both of interest. The composer Ravel lived here.

WHAT TO SEE...

To the west, the fine 17th century château at Fleury-la-Forêt, to the south the evocative ruins of the 12th century Abbaye de Mortemer (plus museum) and to the south-west the Abbaye de Fontaine-Guérard, of a similar period and condition.

WHAT TO LOOK OUT FOR ...

Foie gras and pâté (made for more than 75 years with poultry liver, pork and port).

WHERE TO GO FOR...

FOIE GRAS & PÂTÉ
Patrick Duguet, Maître Charcutier, Lyons-la-Forêt. Tel: 32.49.60.68.

WHERE TO EAT...

La Renaissance, 109 rue Pouyer-Quertier, Fleury-sur-Andelle, nr Lyons-la-Forêt. Tel: 32.49.00.57.

Les Andelys

Both the town and the River Seine, which flows past, are dominated by the splendid ruins of Château Gaillard, the pride of Richard Coeur de Lion who ordered its construction at the end of the 11th century, but which King John later managed to lose to the French crown. In the 6th century there was a monastery here, founded by Clotilde. A fountain, on the site where she is said to have turned water into wine, bears her name.

WHAT TO SEE ...

Château Gaillard, Eglise Notre-Dame (originating from the 13th century) and Eglise Saint-Sauveur (with a late 17th century organ).

WHERE TO GO FOR...

CIDER
Eric Doré, Domaine de Frenelles, Saint-Jean-de-Frenelles, nr Les Andelys. Tel: 32.69.41.25.

GOAT'S CHEESE
Stéphane Langui, Ferme de Criquetuit, 117 route de Bonnemare, Bacqueville, nr Les Andelys. Tel: 32.49.54.27.

FOIE GRAS
P Van Tornhout, 11 rue Pierre Simon, Guiseniers, nr Les Andelys. Also poultry. Tel: 32.54.06.62.

WHERE TO EAT & STAY ...

La Chaîne d'Or, 27 rue Grande, Les Andelys. Tel: 32.54.00.31.

Le Manoir de Clairval, Le Thuit, Le Val-Saint-Martin, nr Les Andelys. Tel: 32.54.00.60.

Le Moulin de Connelles, 40 route d'Amfreville-sous-les-Monts, Connelles, nr Les Andelys. Tel: 32.59.53.33.

Gaillon

Here the castle, perched on a cliff overlooking the Seine, is the main feature. It was built at the end of the 15th century by France's first great cardinal-minister, Georges d'Amboise. Sadly it was stripped of its treasures during the Revolution.

WHERE TO GO FOR ...

FOIE GRAS
Philippe Leber, Les Noës, Saint-Aubin-sur-Gaillon, nr Gaillon. Also cider. Tel: 32.53.06.80.

POULTRY
Alain Desvignes, Habloville, Saint-Aubin-sur-Gaillon, nr Gaillon. Tel: 32.53.06.60.

FRUIT & VEGETABLES
Patrick Delahaye, Le Hazey, Vieux-Villez, nr Gaillon. Tel: 32.53.41.99.

WHERE TO EAT ...

Auberge du Roi-Richard, 26 rue de la Gare, La Mare-sous-Venables, nr Gaillon. Tel: 32.53.31.39.

Relais de l'Ours, N15, Fontaine-Bellenger, nr Gaillon. Tel: 32.53.43.30.

WHERE TO EAT & STAY ...

Hostellerie du Clos Corneille, Vieux-Villez, nr Gaillon. Tel: 32.53.88.00.

Hôtel Les 3 Saint-Pierre, N15, Le Goulet, nr Gaillon. Tel:32.52.50.61.

Les 4 Ecluses, Notre-Dame-de-la-Garenne, nr Gaillon. Tel: 32.53.01.25.

Les Deux Sapins, Cailly-sur-Eure, La Croix-Saint-Leufroy, nr Gaillon. Tel: 32.67.75.13.

Louviers

Set in the middle of three valleys – those of the Seine, Eure and Iton – the town naturally provides a good centre for anglers. The old part to the north of the 13th century Eglise Notre-Dame will prove of great interest, with its traditional half-timbered houses. Its ancient cloth industry has long since given way to more modern technology.

WHAT TO SEE ...

Eglise Notre-Dame, Maison du Fou du Roy (now the tourist office) and a curious museum of film and theatre sets – the works of Georges Wakhévitch who lived nearby.

WHERE TO GO FOR ...

FOIE GRAS
Annick Metrot, 26 rue Maure, Vraiville, nr Louviers. Tel: 32.50.61.34.

M-F Nas de Tourris, 20 rue du Bois Normand, Vraiville, nr Louviers. Tel: 32.50.62.63.

Michel Lenfant, 7 rue de la Plaine, Saint-Etienne-du-Vauvray, nr Louviers. Also poultry. Tel: 32.61.15.78.

Mireille Wolf, Ferme Sainte-Marguerite, Val-de-Reuil, nr Louviers. Tel: 32.59.66.84.

CIDER
Charles Lelieur, 20 rue de la Mairie, Vraiville, nr Louviers. Tel: 32.50.61.84.

WHERE TO EAT ...

La Fontaine Saint-Gabriel, 2 place de l'Eglise, Lery, nr Louviers. Tel: 32.59.09.39.

Le Clos Normand, Rue de la Gare, Louviers. Tel: 32.40.03.56.

La Louvière, 34 chemin de Halage, Poses, nr Louviers. Tel: 32.59.07.06.

WHERE TO EAT & STAY ...

Le Pré Saint-Germain, 7 rue Saint-Germain, Louviers. Tel: 32.40.48.48.

Hostellerie Saint-Pierre, Saint-Pierre-du-Vauvray, nr Louviers. Tel: 32.59.93.29.

Les Saisons, Route des Saisons, Vironvay, nr Louviers. Tel: 32.40.02.56.

Elbeuf

The town, sited on a loop of the River Seine , was once home to a flourishing textile industry. There are a couple of churches (Saint-Etienne and Saint-Jean) worth a visit, as well as a natural history museum and a much-welcomed and well-wooded park.

WHERE TO GO FOR ...

CIDER ETC.
Alain Caboulet, Les Hauts-Vents, Saint-Ouen-du-Tilleul, nr Elbeuf. Tel: 32.87.70.11.

Maurice Martzel, Rue François Cevert, La Saussaye, nr Elbeuf. Also poultry. Tel: 35.87.81.30.

Le 1900, 33 rue Guynemer, Elbeuf.
Tel: 35.77.07.27.

Le Bailliage, 62 route du Pont-de-
l'Arche, Freneuse, nr Elbeuf.
Tel: 35.87.57.37.

L'Hermitage, Maison Brûlée, La
Londe, nr Elbeuf. Tel: 35.18.01.60.

La Fine Auberge, 785 rue Pierre-Gos-
selin, Moulineaux, nr Elbeuf.
Tel: 35.18.02.39.

Le Manoir des Sources, Rue des
Sources, Moulineaux, nr Elbeuf.
Tel: 35.18.08.98.

Le Cottage Normand, 704 avenue du
Circuit, Orival, nr Elbeuf.
Tel: 35.77.09.69.

Au Rendez-vous d'Chasse, Gare de la
Londe, N138, La Londe, nr Elbeuf.
Tel: 35.18.03.39.

Le Progrès, 47 rue Henry, Elbeuf.
Tel: 35.78.42.67.

Le Manoir des Saules, 2 place Saint-
Martin, La Saussaye, nr Elbeuf.
Tel: 35.87.25.65.

Le Relais des Deux-Marches, 1551
route de Louviers, Saint-Pierre-les-
Elbeuf, nr Elbeuf. Tel: 35.77.28.76.

Rouen

The capital of Haute Normandie is probably best known for the trial and eventual burning at the stake of Joan of Arc in Place du Vieux Marché in 1431. It is also one of France's main ports, despite its inland river location. Based on the north bank of the Seine, the old town is a tourist's dream – full of fascination, elegant and varied architecture, charming narrow streets and a range of spectacular sights. Not least among these is the Gothic cathedral (Notre-Dame) of essentially 13th century origin, which is still undergoing restoration following the legacy of the last war. There are literally hundreds of examples of tradi-tional half-timbered buildings in this part of Rouen. Suffice it to mention just a few streets where the best can be seen – Rue Saint-Romain, Rue Martainville, Rue Damiette, Rue des Bons-Enfants and Rue Eau-de-Robec. Perhaps the most typical is the Rue du Gros-Horloge, which runs from the cathedral to Place du Vieux Marché. Here you will find the Great Clock, magnificently set in an equally impressive archway. Among the many churches, that of Saint-Ouen is particularly out-standing.

WHAT TO SEE …

In addition to the above, here is just a selection of visits: Palais de Justice, Hôtel de Bourgtheroulde, Tour Jeanne d'Arc and a handful of museums – des Beaux-Arts, de la Céramique, Le Secq des Tournelles (wrought ironwork), Jeanne d'Arc, Flaubert (medicine) and des Antiquités de la Seine-Maritime. There are others! To the south-east of the town, La Côte Sainte-Catherine offers a breathtaking view of Rouen, particularly at sun-set, and another can be found at the basilica in Bonsecours.

Duckling (*Caneton à la Rouennaise*) and *Sucre de pomme*. International festival in November. Special market for foie gras at the beginning of June. Also chocolates.

WHERE TO GO FOR:

CHOCOLATES
Anzou, 163 rue du Gros-Horloge, Rouen. Tel: 35.70.59.31.

Beyer, 17 rue Grand-Pont, Rouen. Tel: 35.71.09.36.

Paillard, 32 rue du Gros-Horloge, Rouen. Tel: 35.71.10.15.

Roland, 78 rue des Carmes, Rouen. Tel: 35.71.12.92.

CHARCUTERIE
Le Cochon Qui Dort, 46 rue Armand-Carrel, Rouen. Tel: 35.71.47.37.

FOIE GRAS
Alain Royer, Ferme des Sources, Fontaine-sous-Préaux, nr Rouen. Tel: 35.59.04.58.

Blandine Wittorski, Route de la Mi-Voie, Bosc-Guerard-Saint-Adrien, nr Rouen. Tel: 35.33.20.88.

CALVADOS ETC.
Caves Jeanne-d'Arc, 31 rue Jeanne-d'Arc, Rouen. Tel: 35.71.28.92.

CIDER
Cidrerie de l'Ermitage, 2867 route des Andelys, La Neuville-Chant-d'Oisel, nr Rouen. Tel: 35.79.98.04.

Cidrerie Pontreue, 98 rue de Reims, Rouen. Tel: 35.71.28.27.

Hautecoeur, 15 rue Frédéric-Bérat, Petit-Quevilly, nr Rouen. Tel: 35.72.47.90.

J-P Lambard, Le Quesnay, Pissy Pôville, nr Rouen. Tel: 35.91.51.08.

CHEESE
La Fromagerie, 30 boulevard d'Orléans, Rouen. Also cider, calvados & other regional products. Tel: 35.63.54.00.

Jollit, Place du Vieux-Marché, Rouen. Also cider. Tel: 35.88.72.13.

Leroux, 40 rue de l'Hôpital, Rouen. Also dairy produce & charcuterie. Tel: 35.71.10.40.

Maison Harlé, 18 rue Rollon, Rouen. Tel: 35.71.68.85.

GOAT'S CHEESE
T Breemeersch, 88 rue du Boc, La Neuville-Chant-d'Oisel, nr Rouen. Tel: 35.79.81.24.

Nadine & Christophe Thierry-Voreux, Ferme de Beaulieu, Bois-l'Evêque, nr Rouen. Also vegetables. Tel: 35.23.57.43.

DAIRY PRODUCE
Bernard Gois, 26 route de Duclair, Saint-Jean-du-Cardonnay, nr Rouen. Also poultry & vegetables. Tel: 35.33.81.25.

Jean & Evelyne Bernard, 78 rue de Bas, Saint-Pierre-de-Manneville, nr Rouen. Tel: 35.32.07.13.

TROUT
Pisciculture, Chemin des Sondres, Montville, nr Rouen. Tel: 35.33.71.74.

VEGETABLES
F-B de Keating-Hart, Rue de la Bucaille, Quincampoix, nr Rouen. Also strawberries. Tel: 35.34.77.42.

Katherine Berry, Ferme de Saint-Maurice, Malaunay, nr Rouen. Also fruit and dried flowers. Tel: 35.75.24.45.

POTTERY ETC.
Au Vieux Rouen, 44 rue de la Tour-de-Beurre, Rouen. Tel: 35.70.54.36.

Bultel, 28 rue de la Tour-de-Beurre, Rouen. Tel: 35.70.54.36.

Fernette, 11 place Barthélémi, Rouen. Tel: 35.70.75.62.

Galerie Cauchoise, 29 rue Cauchoise, Rouen. Tel: 35.71.51.95.

Madame Carpentier, 26 rue Saint-Romain, Rouen. Tel: 35.88.77.47.

Ma Normandie, 48-50 rue Saint-Nicholas, Rouen. Tel: 35.71.46.08.

Rouen Faïence, 56 place du Vieux-Marché, Rouen. Tel: 35.71.58.34.

WHERE TO EAT ...

Gill, 9 quai de la Bourse, Rouen. Tel: 35.71.16.14.

L'Ecaille, 26 rampe Cauchoise, Rouen. Tel: 35.70.95.52.

Auberge du Vieux-Carré, 34 rue Ganterie, Rouen. Tel: 35.71.67.70.

Au Bois Chenu, 23-25 place de la Pucelle-d'Orléans, Rouen. Tel: 35.71.19.54.

La Couronne, 31 place du Vieux-Marché, Rouen. Tel: 35.71.40.90.

Dufour, 67 rue Saint-Micholas, Rouen. Tel: 35.71.90.62.

Le Maupassant, 39 place du Vieux-Marché, Rouen. Tel: 35.07.56.90.

Les Nymphéas, 7-9 Rue de la Pie, Rouen. Tel: 35.89.26.69.

La Rouennais, 5 rue de la Pie, Rouen. Tel: 35.07.55.44.

La Toque d'Or, 11 place du Vieux-Marché, Rouen. Tel: 35.71.46.29.

L'Episode, 37 rue aux Ours, Rouen. Tel: 35.89.01.91.

Pascaline, 5 rue de la Poterne, Rouen. Tel: 35.89.67.44.

La Brasserie des Deux-Rives, La Gare, Rouen. Tel: 35.71.48.66.

Brasserie Paul, 1 place de la Cathédrale, Rouen. Tel: 35.71.86.07.

Pascal Saunier, 12 rue du Belvédère, Mont-Saint-Aignan, nr Rouen. Tel: 35.71.61.06.

Auberge La Grillade, D928, Quincampoix, nr Rouen. Tel: 35.34.70.11.

La Butte, 69 route de Paris, Bonsecours, nr Rouen. Tel: 35.80.43.11.

Les Gastronomes, La Bouille, nr Rouen. Tel: 35.18.02.07.

Auberge du Canard Bleu, Rue des 2 Communes, Port-Saint-Ouen, nr Rouen. Tel: 35.23.65.65.

WHERE TO EAT & STAY ...

Hôtel de Dieppe (L), Place Bernard-Tissot, Rouen. Tel: 35.71.96.00.

Hôtel Ibis (M), 56 quai Gaston-Boulet, Rouen. Tel: 35.70.48.18.

Les Relais Bleus (M), 14 quai Gaston-Boulet, Rouen. Tel: 35.15.25.25.

Hôtel Boieldieu (B), 14 place du Gaillardbois, Rouen. Tel: 35.70.50.75.

La Bonne Marmite (L), 10 rue René-Raban, Pont-Saint-Pierre, nr Rouen. Tel: 32.49.70.24.

WHERE TO STAY ...

Hôtel Mercure (L), Rue Crois-de-Fer, Rouen. Tel: 35.52.69.52.

Colin's Hôtel (L), 15 rue de la Pie, Rouen. Tel: 35.71.00.88.

Hôtel de la Cathédrale (M), 12 rue Saint-Romain, Rouen. Tel: 31.71.57.95.

Le Saint-Pierre (M), Place du Bateau, La Bouille, nr Rouen. Tel: 35.18.01.01.

A busy little town on the main Rouen-Dieppe axis. The main attraction lies to the south – at Clères. For three-quarters of a century a zoo has occupied the grounds of the château, built on the site of an 11th century castle of which a few ruins remain. The natural setting for birds and animals is delightful. There is an interesting covered market in the main square and some marvellous old cars in the Musée de l'Automobile et Militaire.

WHERE TO GO FOR ...

FOIE GRAS
Damien Pesquet, La Ferme du Nisbourg, Bertrimont, nr Tôtes. Tel: 35.32.14.89.

FRUIT
Marc Bouquet, Le Marouin, Biville-la-Baignarde, nr Tôtes. Tel: 35.32.88.86.

GOAT'S CHEESE ETC
Corinne Bourgeaux, L'Epinay, Saint-Maclou-de-Folleville, nr Tôtes. Tel: 35.32.67.07.

WHERE TO EAT ...

Auberge du Cygne, Carrefour de l'Europe, Tôtes. Tel: 35.32.92.03.

Bacqueville-en-Caux

WHERE TO GO FOR ...

FOIE GRAS
Régis Pienoel, Le Mont Candont, Bacqueville-en-Caux. Tel: 35.85.47.02.

Olivier Douville, Notre-Dame, Canville-les-Deux-Eglises, nr Bacqueville-en-Caux. Tel: 35.96.65.42.

FRUIT
Ferme Fruitière, Bois Robert, Longueville-sur-Scie, nr Bacqueville-en-Caux. Also vegetables. Tel: 34.04.41.02.

FARM PRODUCE
Henri & Marie-Thérèse Duramé, Calnon, nr Bacqueville-en-Caux. Also rooms. Tel: 35.85.41.41.

RABBIT PRODUCTS
Patrick & Sylvie Pecqueur, Le Pelletôt, Le Catelier, nr Bacqueville-en-Caux. Also angora wool. Tel: 35.04.61.76.

Samuel & Françoise Mordant, La Ferme Cauchoise, Hameau des Mesnils, Lammerville, nr Bacqueville-en-Caux. Tel: 35.83.28.76.

WHERE TO EAT ...

Restaurant de Paris, Route de Paris, Torcy-le-Grand, nr Bacqueville-en-Caux. Tel: 35.85.58.03.

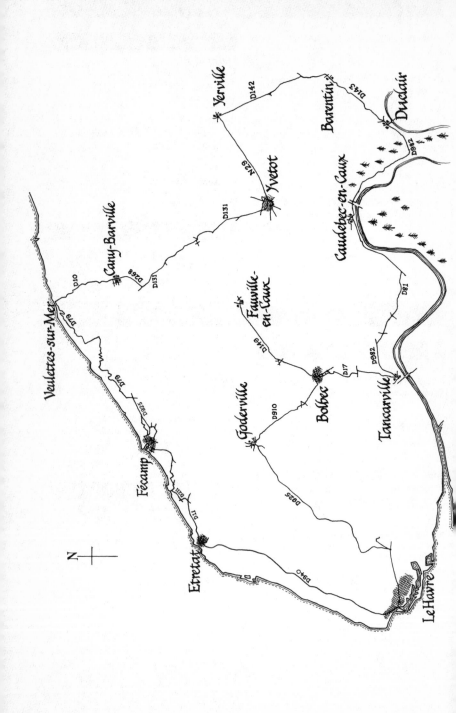

Pays de Caux

This route, which begins at Le Havre, takes you along the Alabaster Coast, where the chalk cliffs tower mightily above The Channel. The views are at times quite breathtaking. You then turn south into the heart of the Pays de Caux, a fertile chalk plateau punctuated by deep ravines and river valleys. This is agricultural country, characterised by many pretty little farmsteads with their typical half-timbered buildings, as far as the wooded banks of the Seine. After sampling the fascinations of this mighty river, you can enjoy some more of the Caux's rich farmland before returning to Le Havre.

YOUR ROUTE ...

D940 from Le Havre to Etretat.

D11 then D211 to Fécamp.

D925 then D79 to Veulettes-sur-Mer.

D10 to Cany-Barville.

D268 then D131 to Yvetot.

N29 to Yerville.

D142 to Barentin.

D143 to Duclair.

D982 to Caudebec-en-Caux.

D81 then D982 to Tancarville.

D17 to Bolbec.

(D149 to Fauville-en-Caux)

D910 to Goderville.

D925 to Le Havre.

Le Havre

Although one of the arrival ports for cross-Channel passengers, there is really not very much to hold the visitors' attention for long. Although its importance as a major seaport and industrial centre is undisputed, probably only those interested in post-war urban development and architecture would really appreciate an extensive tour. The old town was virtually destroyed in the 11 days it took the Allies to liberate Le Havre in September 1944. However the cathedral (as was often the case) still stands, along with some of the original buildings. Other parts meriting a visit include the Bassin du Roy, along with the Saint-Vincent quarter. This quaint corner has some interesting little shops.

Your route out from Le Havre has recently been made much easier and quicker – particularly for those heading west and south-west – by the opening of the magnificent Pont de Normandie, which spans the Seine Estuary.

WHAT TO SEE ...

The large Place de l'Hôtel de Ville, Avenue Foch, the inside of L'Eglise Saint-Joseph and the very original fine arts museum – Musée des Beaux-Arts André Malraux. Of more traditional interest there is the 16th century Cathédrale Notre-Dame, Abbaye de Graville (with museum), Musée de l'Ancien Havre and Forêt de Montgeon. Just to the north is the resort of Sainte-Adresse, where the Belgian government was based during the last war. There are some fine villas – and views, particularly from the fort and Cap de la Hève. To the east, Château d'Orcher near Gonfreville – in Louis XV style – is worth a visit.

WHERE TO GO FOR ...

CHOCOLATES
Square Delices, 76 rue Frédéric-Bellanger, Saint-Vincent, Le Havre. Tel: 35.21.31.24.

Philippe Bosquer, 106 avenue René-Coty, Le Havre. Tel: 35.41.28.19.

CIDER ETC.
La Maison des Vins, 59 rue Jules Tellier, Le Havre. Tel: 35.25.39.73.

DAIRY PRODUCE & FRUIT
Au P'tit Normand, 71 bis rue Casimir-Delavigne, Danton, Le Havre. Tel: 35.21.34.18.

SHELLFISH ETC.
Poissonnerie Virel, 41-43 rue de Paris, Le Havre. Tel: 35.42.46.33.

Poissonerie Normande, 243 rue Aristide-Briand, Le Havre. Tel: 35.41.24.93.

ALL FARM PRODUCE
Les Huit Fermes, Gonfreville-l'Orcher, nr Le Havre. Tel: 35.20.61.25.

WHERE TO EAT ...

Athanor, 120 rue Guillemard, Le Havre. Tel: 35.42.50.27.

La Toque, 80 rue de Verdun, Graville, Le Havre. Tel: 35.47.86.06.

Le Cardinal, 107 boulevard de Strasbourg, Le Havre. Tel: 35.43.45.45.

Le Gallieni, 66 rue Maréchal-Gallieni, Le Havre. Tel: 35.41.22.50.

Le Petit Bedon, 37-39 rue Louis-Brindeau, Le Havre. Tel: 35.41.36.81.

Le Nossi Bé, 50-52 quai Michel-Féré, Le Havre. Tel: 35.42.77.44.

A L'Entrecôte, 23 rue Buffon, Le Havre. Tel: 35.25.12.47.

Les Gastronomes, 24 rue Dauphine, Le Havre. Tel: 35.43.17.22.

C Cottard, Le Beaucamp, Saint-Aubin-Routot, nr Le Havre. Must book.
Tel: 35.20.52.01.

Yveline Toumine, Le Mesnil, Montivilliers, nr Le Havre. Must book.
Tel: 35.30.13.85.

Restaurant Yves Page, 7 place Clémenceau, Sainte-Adresse, nr Le Havre. Tel: 35.46.06.09.

Restaurant Bures, Rue Félix-Faure, Octeville-sur-Mer, nr Le Havre.
Tel: 35.46.36.39.

Les Hautes Vallées, Octeville-sur-Mer, nr Le Havre. Tel: 35.48.68.17.

La Fontaine Fleurie, Avenue Jean-Jaurès, Fontaine-la-Mallet, nr Le Havre.
Tel: 35.20.10.00.

Hôtel Mercure (L), Chaussée d'Angoulême, Le Havre. Tel: 35.19.50.50.

Hôtel Astoria (M), 13 cours de la République, Le Havre. Tel: 35.25.00.03.

Hôtel France Bourgogne (M), 19-21 cour de la République, Le Havre.
Tel: 35.25.40.34.

Le Monaco (M), 16 rue de Paris, Le Havre. Tel: 35.42.21.01.

Les Relais Bleus (M), Quai Colbert, Le Havre. Tel: 35.26.49.49.

L'Ecureuil (B), 104 avenue de Frileuse, Le Havre. Tel: 35.47.20.78.

Hôtel Campanile (M), ZA du Camp-Dolent, Gonfreville-l'Orcher, nr Le Havre. Tel: 35.51.43.00.

Hôtel Climat (M), ZA La Lézarde, Montivilliers, nr Le Havre.
Tel: 35.30.41.39.

Etretat

This seaside resort is famed for its cliffs which make up one of the most dramatic sections of coastline in the whole of Normandy. Not to be missed are La Falaise d'Aval, La Falaise d'Amont and – the most famous landmark – L'Aiguille d'Etretat, the needle-shaped rock standing solitarily just offshore. In the town itself, there is a wooden covered market in Place du Maréchal-Foch and some pleasant timber-framed houses in Boulevard Président-René-Coty. Following the coast to the southwest there is a fine view from Cap d'Antifer, particularly the lighthouse.

GOAT'S CHEESE
Le Valaine, Manoir de Cateuil, Route du Havre, Etretat. Tel: 35.27.14.02.

HONEY
Les Ruchers d'Etretat, Ferme des Platanes, Bordeaux-Saint-Clair, nr Etretat. Tel: 35.28.82.36.

La Belle Epoque, Boulevard René-Coty, Etretat. Tel: 35.28.83.74.

Le Bicorne, 5 boulevard René-Coty, Etretat. Tel: 35.29.62.22.

Le Belvédère, Saint-Jouin-Bruneval, nr Etretat. Tel: 35.20.13.76.

Le Donjon, Chemin de Saint-Clair, Etretat. Tel: 35.27.08.23.

Hôtel Saint-Christophe, Le Tilleul, Etretat. Tel: 35.28.84.29.

Fécamp

This busy little fishing port, from where boats sail to Newfoundland in search of cod, is also home of the famous liqueur Benedictine, and the writer Guy de Maupassant once lived here. Local activities include the drying of cod and the curing of herrings. Notable sights include a museum devoted to the maritime past (Musée des Terres-Neuvas et de la Pêche) and one to local art (Musée Centre-des-Arts). Le Palais Bénédictine is a must for those interested in the background and production of the unique liqueur, and L'Eglise de la Trinité, dating from the 12th century, is also worth a visit.

WHAT TO SEE ...

Palais Bénédictine, Eglise de la Trinité, Musée des Terres-Neuvas et de la Pêche and Musée Centre-des-Arts. Heading north-east, you will get a magnificent view of the coastline near the chapel of Notre-Dame-du-Salut. Inland, to the east, Valmont is dominated by its castle and the ruins of a Benedictine abbey.

WHAT TO LOOK OUT FOR ...

Benedictine liqueur and fish, most particularly cod and mackerel.

WHERE TO GO FOR ...

BENEDICTINE
Palais Bénédictine, Rue Alexandre-le-Grand, Fécamp. Tel: 35.10.26.00.

DAIRY PRODUCE
Jean-Marie Dutot, Saint-Léonard, Fécamp. Also vegetables.
Tel: 35.28.28.80.

FARM PRODUCE
Dominique & Sylvie Leplay, Sainte-Hélène-Bondeville, nr Fécamp.
Tel: 35.28.17.51.

WHERE TO EAT ...

Le Viking, 63 boulevard Albert 1er, Fécamp. Tel: 35.29.22.92.

Le Maritime, 2 place Nicholas-Selle, Fécamp. Tel: 35.28.21.71.

La Plaisance, 33-35 quai Vicomté, Fécamp. Tel: 35.29.38.14.

Le Relais des Dalles, Sassetot-le-Malconduit, nr Fécamp. Tel: 35.27.41.83.

Auberge du Bec-au-Cauchois, Route de Fécamp, Valmont, nr Fécamp.
Tel: 35.29.77.56.

Ferme Auberge de la Côte-d'Albâtre, Criquebeuf-en-Caux, nr Fécamp. Must book. Tel: 35.28.01.32.

Auberge du Fond-Pitron, Saint-Léonard, nr Fécamp. Tel: 35.27.33.53.

This small town on the banks of the River Durdent has an attractive church with some fine carved panelling. Just to the south is Cany Château, dating from the reign of Louis XIII, whose moats are fed by the same river.

WHERE TO GO FOR...

DUCK & POULTRY
La Ferme d'Artemare, Saint-Vaast-Dieppedalle, nr Cany-Barville.
Tel: 35.96.57.41.

FRUIT
Sabine Haquet, Hameau de Ruville, Bosville, nr Cany-Barville.
Tel: 35.97.70.74.

WHERE TO EAT ...

L'Auberge de France, 73 rue du Général-de-Gaulle, Cany-Barville.
Tel: 35.97.80.10.

WHERE TO EAT & STAY ...

Le Manoir de Barville, Cany-Barville.
Tel: 35.97.79.30.

This popular seaside resort, with both commercial and leisure harbours, has impressive headlands to either side – Falaise d'Aval to the west and Falaise d'Amont to the east. Both have war monuments. Look out for the fine Renaissance-style Maison Henri IV in Quai du Havre.

WHAT TO LOOK OUT FOR ...

Lobsters.

WHERE TO GO FOR ...

FARM PRODUCE
Jean-François & Catherine Bocquet, Houdetot, nr Saint-Valery-en-Caux.
Tel: 35.97.08.73.

WHERE TO EAT ...

Les Embruns, Place de l'Eglise, Sotteville-sur-Mer, nr Saint-Valery-en-Caux. Tel: 35.97.77.99.

Auberge du Dun, Route de Dieppe, Bourg Dun, nr Saint-Valery-en-Caux.
Tel: 35.83.05.84.

Les Galets, Veules-les-Roses-Plage, nr Saint-Valery-en-Caux. Tel: 35.97.61.33.

WHERE TO EAT & STAY ...

Les Frégates/Les Bains, Veulettes-sur-Mer, nr Saint-Valery-en-Caux.
Tel: 35.97.51.22.

WHERE TO STAY ...

Les Hêtres, Rue des Fleurs, Le Bourg, Ingouville-sur-Mer, nr Saint-Valery-en-Caux. Tel: 35.57.09.30.

Yvetot

This important regional market town boasts some fine stained-glass windows in its church (Saint-Pierre). Notice the typical Caux farmhouses in the area and take a look at the most famous tree in Normandy – a 1300-year-old oak at Allouville-Bellefosse, just to the south west. There is also an interesting nature museum nearby.

WHAT TO LOOK OUT FOR ...

Cider, *pommeau, eau-de-vie* and duck. Also special market for foie gras from mid-November to early December.

WHERE TO GO FOR ...

CIDER ETC.
Le Verger d'Augustin, La Folletière, nr Yvetot. Also rooms.Tel: 35.91.19.20.

Benoît Lemercier, Flamanville, Motteville, nr Yvetot. Tel: 35.96.85.70.

DAIRY PRODUCE
Jocelyn Pesqueux, Allouville-Bellefosse, nr Yvetot. Tel: 35.96.03.59.

GOAT'S CHEESE
Alain Rivière, Chèvrerie-de-Saint-Cosme, Etoutteville, nr Yvetot. Tel: 35.56.95.26.

GENERAL FARM PRODUCE
Les Vergers de Runetot, Croixmare, nr Yvetot. Also linen. Tel: 35.92.72.11.

TROUT
Pisciculture de la Durdent, Héricourt-en-Caux, nr Yvetot. Tel: 35.96.51.88.

PIGEON
Claude Pellerin, Valliquerville, nr Yvetot. Tel: 35.95.00.75.

WHERE TO EAT ...

Au Bon Roy d'Yvetot, 70 rue Bellanger, Yvetot. Tel: 35.95.19.75.

Au Bon Saint-Bernard, 1 avenue Maréchal Foch, Yvetot. Tel: 35.95.06.75.

La Pergola, 52 avenue Clemenceau, Yvetot. Tel: 35.95.08.13.

Auberge La Maison Normande, Route de Rouen, N15, Yvetot. Tel: 35.56.50.38.

WHERE TO STAY ...

L'Auberge du Val-au-Cesne, Le Val-au-Cesne, nr Yvetot. Tel: 35.56.63.06.

Yerville

WHERE TO GO FOR ...

HONEY
Michel Clatot, Hameau de Becquigny, Limesy, nr Yerville. Tel: 35.91.19.97.

WHERE TO EAT ...

L'Hostellerie des Voyageurs, Rue Jacques-Ferny, Yerville. Tel: 35.96.82.55.

A M Cavelan, Boucourt, Benesville, nr Yerville. Must book. Tel: 35.96.55.99.

The quayside of this busy little town, which is famed for its delicious duck, has a pleasant if somewhat incongruous setting with heavy cargo steaming up and down the River Seine in the heart of the countryside. Of particular note here is the 12th century belfry of the church (Saint-Denis).

WHAT TO SEE ...

Following the Seine as it weaves its way gradually westwards, you will reach the impressive Norman abbey ruins at Jumièges, the most outstanding section of which is L'Eglise Notre-Dame. The drive, best done at apple-blossom time, takes you via Le Mesnil-sous-Jumièges and its 13th century manor.

WHAT TO LOOK OUT FOR ...

Duck. Also poultry and fruit.

WHERE TO GO FOR ...

DUCK
Robert Maugard, La Ferme du Canardier, Anneville-Ambourville, nr Duclair. Tel: 35.37.56.41.

FRUIT
Patrick Sadones, Le Conihout, Le Mesnil-sous-Jumièges, nr Duclair. Also goat's cheese. Tel: 35.37.35.08.

Nadine Armeli, Le Conihout, Jumièges, nr Duclair. Tel: 35.37.95.12.

Jacqueline Cheron, Anneville-Ambourville, nr Duclair. Tel: 35.37.53.36.

Robert Decaux, Lieudit-le-Port, Yville-sur-Seine, nr Duclair. Tel: 35.37.57.86.

Earl Demoy, La Grange Dîmière, Heurteauville, nr Duclair. Also eau-de-vie. Tel: 35.37.10.17.

Michel Guilbert, Chemin du Halage, Le Mesnil-sous-Jumièges, nr Duclair. Tel: 35.37.74.42.

Gilbert Landrin, Route du Mesnil, Jumièges, nr Duclair. Also vegetables. Tel: 35.37.27.29.

Eric Lefebvre, Route des Marais, Anneville-Ambourville, nr Duclair. Tel: 35.37.00.21.

HONEY
Le Monde Merveilleux des Abeilles, Le Halage, Le Mesnil-sous-Jumièges, nr Duclair. Also foie gras & cider. Tel: 35.37.32.44.

WHERE TO EAT ...

Le Parc, 721 avenue du Président-Coty, Duclair. Tel: 35.37.50.31.

Le Ronceray, Sainte-Marguerite-sur-Duclair, nr Duclair. Must book. Tel: 35.37.53.02.

Auberge de la Mare au Coq, Route de Mesnil, Jumièges, nr Duclair. Must book. Tel: 35.37.43.57.

La Fauconnerie, Blacqueville, nr Duclair. Must book. Tel: 35.92.19.41.

Claude Quesnel, Goupillières, Pavilly, nr Duclair. Must book. Tel: 35.91.02.83.

WHERE TO STAY ...

Auberge des Ruines, Place de la Mairie, Jumièges, nr Duclair. Tel: 35.37.24.05.

Caudebec-en-Caux

Strategically sited on the banks of the Seine, the town has played its part in various chapters of French history. Built in the form of an amphitheatre, it was ravaged by fire in 1940. Happily the fine Eglise Notre-Dame survived, along with some nearby houses. The fine 'golden' Pont de Brotonne dominates the landscape here.

WHAT TO SEE ...

Eglise Notre-Dame, Maison des Templiers, Musée de la Marine de Seine, the old prison and La Place du Marché, where the market has been held since 1390. Saturday is the time to visit. To the east is Saint-Wandrille-Rançon with its imposing Benedictine abbey, where the monks now produce – amongst other things – furniture polish. Of particular interest are the monumental gateway, Porte de Jarente, the cloisters and the church housed in an original 13th century tithe barn. Travelling west – downstream – from Caudebec-en-Caux, the village of Villequier contains Le Musée Victor Hugo. It was here that Hugo's daughter and son-in-law were drowned. Further south Château Etelan provides an imposing sight.

WHERE TO GO FOR ...

CIDER
Jacques Feuillye, Route de Chaumières, Notre-Dame-de-Bliquetuit, nr Caudebec-en-Caux. Tel: 35.96.27.45.

FOIE GRAS
François Grenon, Bourg Corblin, Notre-Dame-de-Bliquetuit, nr Caudebec-en-Caux. Tel: 35.37.18.10.

J-C Dolique, Hameau-le-Genetay, Saint-Wandrille-Rançon, nr Caudebec-en-Caux. Also poultry. Tel: 35.96.42.00.

TROUT
Marc Genet, Saint-Wandrille-Rançon, nr Caudebec-en-Caux. Tel: 35.96.36.98.

HONEY
Pilate Apiculture, Rue de l'Oiseau Bleu, Saint-Wandrille-Rançon, nr Caudebec-en-Caux. Tel: 35.96.17.75.

WHERE TO EAT ...

Le Manoir de Rétival, Caudebec-en-Caux. Tel: 35.96.11.22.

Les Deux Couronnes, Saint-Wandrille-Rançon, nr Caudebec-en-Caux. Tel: 35.96.11.44.

La Bergerie, Saint-Arnoult, nr Caudebec-en-Caux. Must book. Tel: 35.56.75.84.

WHERE TO STAY ...

Auberge au Grand Méchant Loup, Louvetot, nr Caudebec-en-Caux. Tel: 35.95.46.56.

Normotel La Marine, 18 quai Guilbaud, Caudebec-en-Caux. Tel: 35.96.20.11.

La Normandie, 19 quai Guilbaud, Caudebec-en-Caux. Tel: 35.96.25.11.

Auberge de Norville, Rue des Ecoles, Norville, nr Caudebec-en-Caux. Tel: 35.39.91.14.

Tancarville

The opening of the Pont de Normandie has relieved the traffic on the mighty suspension bridge here – one of the largest in Europe – which used to take all the traffic crossing the lower reaches of the Seine. Somewhat dwarfed by such a lofty neighbour is the feudal castle, of 10th century origin, the main feature of which is Le Tour de l'Aigle.

FRUIT
Isabelle Lefrançois, Ferme de l'Epine, Saint-Vigor-d'Ymonville, nr Tancarville. Tel: 35.20.98.78.

L'Auberge des Falaises, Le Hode, D982, Saint-Vigor-d'Ymonville, nr Tancarville. Tel: 35.20.06.97.

La Chaumière, 10 rue du Village, Saint-Maurice-d'Etelan, nr Tancarville. Tel: 35.39.91.28.

Restaurant La Forge, D39, La Cerlangue, nr Tancarville. Tel: 35.20.50.54.

La Marine, Tancarville. Tel: 35.39.77.15.

La P'tite Auberge, 20 rue du Havre, Lillebonne, nr Tancarville. Tel: 35.38.00.59.

Bolbec

TROUT
Henri Barray, 15 rue Fond Vallée, Lillebonne, nr Bolbec. Tel: 35.38.04.76.

Le Saint-Thomas, 76 avenue Maréchal-Foch, Gruchet-la-Valasse, nr Bolbec. Tel: 35.31.85.22.

Hôtel Promotour, 113 avenue du Maréchal-Joffre, Bolbec. Tel: 35.31.88.89.

Fauville-en-Caux

CIDER
Gérard Benoist, Angerville-Bailleul, nr Fauville-en-Caux. Tel: 35.27.70.30.

HONEY
J-M Ledoux, Hameau-de-la-Foye, Normanville, nr Fauville-en-Caux. Tel: 35.29.50.95.

DAIRY PRODUCE
Bernard & Michèle Eudes, Hameau de Trois-Fermes, Bennetot, nr Fauville-en-Caux. Tel: 35.96.77.89.

Jacques & Françoise Le Ber, Ferme du Calvaire, Normanville, nr Fauville-en-Caux. Tel: 35.27.60.05.

Au Moulin à Grains, Trouville-Alliquerville, nr Fauville-en-Caux. Tel: 35.38.04.46.

Auberge de la Durdent, Route de Cany, Hericourt-en-Caux, nr Fauville-en-Caux. Tel: 35.96.42.44.

Goderville

FOIE GRAS
Pierrette Thomas, Ecrainville, nr Goderville. Tel: 35.27.39.74.

Gérard Dureçu, Anglesqueville-l'Esneval, nr Goderville. Tel: 35.20.72.75.

Hôtel de Fécamp, Hameau de la Gare, Bréauté, nr Goderville. Tel: 35.38.62.21.

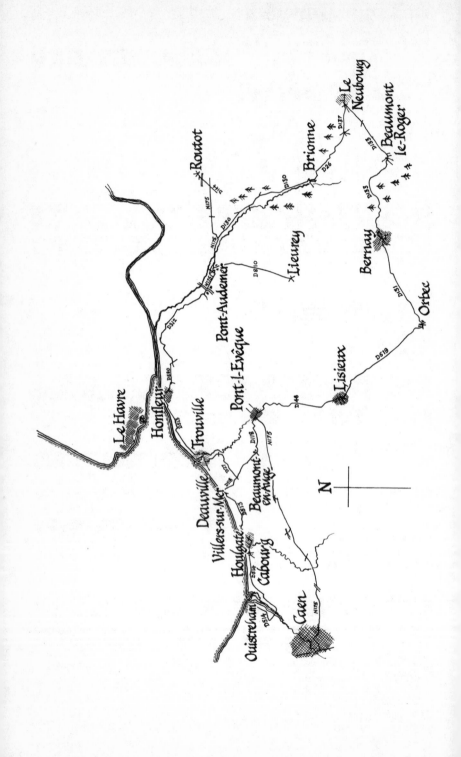

Discovering the
Pays d'Auge

This tour, which begins from Ouistreham, runs first along the Côte Fleurie, whose name will gain a clear meaning as you drive from one elegant and colourful resort to another. To the south lies the Pays d'Auge, with its rural manor houses and pretty thatched cottages. Here orchards and grazing land abound – and no wonder, therefore, that the principal products here include cider, Calvados and cheese. The round trip takes you through some of the prettiest parts of Normandy – wooded valleys with small towns almost lost in them – before bringing you back to the coast.

YOUR ROUTE ...

D514 from Ouistreham to Cabourg.

D513 to Houlgate & Villers-sur-Mer.

D118 then D27 to Deauville & Trouville.

D513 to Honfleur.

D580, D312 then N175 to Pont-Audemer.

(N175 then D144 to Routot)

(D810 to Lieurey)

N175 then D130 to Brionne.

D26 then D137 to Le Neubourg.

D133 to Beaumont-le-Roger & Bernay.

D131 to Orbec.

D519 to Lisieux.

D48 to Pont-l'Evêque.

D118 to Beaumont-en-Auge & Villers-sur-Mer.
(or N175 to Caen & Ouistreham)

Ouistreham

One of the ports of arrival for ferries from Portsmouth, this town lies at the mouth of the Orne river and canal which both lead to Caen. Serving fishing boats as well as leisure craft, it also offers a fine beach at Riva Bella – created from the ruins left after the Allied Invasion in 1944. A museum commemorates the events. There is an interesting 12th century fortress church – Saint-Samson – and fine views from the top of the lighthouse.

WHERE TO GO FOR ...
POTTERY
Gilbert Lecouturier, Langrune-sur-Mer, nr Ouistreham. Tel: 31.96.86.40.

WHERE TO EAT ...
Luc Joignant, Bénouville, nr Ouistreham. Tel: 31.44.62.26.

La Ferme Saint-Hubert, 3 rue de la Mer, Colleville-Montgomery Bourg, nr Ouistreham. Tel: 31.96.35.41.

WHERE TO STAY ...
Le Normandie, 71 avenue Michel-Cabieu, Ouistreham Port. Tel: 31.97.19.57.

La Glycine, Bénouville, nr Ouistreham. Tel: 31.44.61.94.

Cabourg

This seaside resort with extensive yachting facilities was the favourite haunt of the French writer Marcel Proust. Its street layout has an interesting symmetry based on the Casino and Grand Hotel. On the eastern side of the estuary is Dives-sur-Mer, with a small fishing harbour and marina. Its main claim to fame is as the port from which William the Conqueror left to invade England in 1066. Here you should visit the impressive oak-framed covered market – Les Halles – which dates from the 15th century. Browse round the art and craft shops of Le Village Guillaume le Conquérant.

WHAT TO SEE ...
To the west, there is a bunker museum at Merville-Franceville Plage to commemorate the Allied landings in 1944, and the village of Ranville, to the south, which was the first to be liberated by the British troops, has a war cemetery. In neighbouring Dives-sur-Mer, the massive Eglise Notre-Dame, 14th century, is worth a call.

WHERE TO GO FOR ...
PASTRIES & CHOCOLATE
Dupont, 73 avenue de la Mer, Cabourg. Tel: 31.24.60.32.

WHERE TO EAT ...
Le Beau Site, Promenade Marcel-Proust, Cabourg. Tel: 31.24.42.88.

Le Romantique, 8 avenue Piat, Cabourg. Tel: 31.24.10.92.

Le Hastings, 2 avenue de la Mer, Cabourg. Tel: 31.24.33.09.

Le Balbec, Promenade Marcel-Proust, Cabourg. Tel: 31.91.01.79.

Chez Le Bougnat, 27 rue Gaston-Manneville, Dives-sur-Mer, nr Cabourg. Tel: 31.91.06.13.

Le Grand Hôtel, Promenade Marcel-Proust, Cabourg. Tel: 31.91.01.79.

Castel Fleuri, 4 avenue Piat, Cabourg. Tel: 31.91.27.57.

Hôtel de la Gare, Route de Cabourg, Merville-Franceville, nr Cabourg. Tel: 31.24.23.37.

L'Auberge des Viviers, 73 avenue Charles de Gaulle, Cabourg. Tel: 31.91.05.10.

Houlgate

This small but charming seaside resort tucked into the Drochon Valley offers the choice of a fine sandy beach and rich green countryside.

WHAT TO LOOK OUT FOR …

Teurgoule, a traditional Normandy rice pudding flavoured with cinnamon. Show in the autumn.

WHERE TO GO FOR …

TEURGOULE
François Lebrun, Ferme de la Bruyère, Heuland, nr Houlgate. Also dairy produce. Tel: 31.79.25.67.

DAIRY PRODUCE
Sabine Houlet, Ferme de l'Oraille, Douville-en-Auge, nr Houlgate. Tel: 31.79.93.43.

WHERE TO EAT …

M R Van Der Brugghe, 44 rue des Bains, Houlgate. Tel: 31.91.22.51.

WHERE TO EAT & STAY …

Auberge de la Ferme des Aulnettes, Route de la Corniche, Houlgate. Tel: 31.28.00.28.

Le Normand, 40 rue du Général-Leclerc, Houlgate. Tel: 31.24.81.81.

Le Calvados, 16 rue Henry Fouchard, Houlgate. Tel: 31.24.80.20.

La Ferme du Lieu Marot, 21 route de la Vallée, Houlgate. Tel: 31.91.19.44.

Villers-sur-Mer

This lively seaside town offers a pleasing mix of beach and woodland. For those interested in fossils, a visit to Le Musée Paléontologique is a must, as is La Falaise des Vaches Noires, cliffs just to the south-west where many of the items displayed were found.

WHAT TO LOOK OUT FOR …

Andouillette, *boudin* and teurgoule.

WHERE TO GO FOR …

ANDOUILLETTE & BOUDIN
Jacques Blavette, Charcutier-Traiteur, A La Renommée, 18 rue du Général de Gaulle, Villers-sur-Mer. Tel: 31.87.04.25.

L'Auberge L'Escale, Place de l'Hôtel de Ville, Blonville-sur-Mer, nr Villers-sur-Mer. Tel: 31.87.93.56.

La Bonne Auberge, 1 rue du Maréchal-Leclerc, Villers-sur-Mer. Tel: 31.87.04.64.

Le Celtic, 18 rue du Maréchal-Leclerc, Villers-sur-Mer. Tel: 31.87.41.46.

Deauville

This glamorous and fashionable resort is the ideal place for those wanting entertainment and who have money to spare. One notable feature is the wooden promenade – Les Planches – the length of the beach (known as La Plage Fleurie), where you can watch all the comings and goings of the rich and famous. There is also a port and a yacht marina. Deauville is well served by two race courses – at La Touques and Clairefontaine. Le Mont Canisy to the south provides a fine viewpoint.

WHAT TO LOOK OUT FOR ...

Crustacea and seafood – *moules à la crème aux crevettes*, crab and lobster. Also calvados.

WHERE TO GO FOR ...

CALVADOS
Bernard Lebey, Ferme de la Croix Solier, Tourgéville, nr Deauville. Tel: 31.88.14.10.

WHERE TO EAT ...

L'Océan, 1 quai de la Marine, Deauville. Tel: 31.88.92.51.

Le Spinnaker, 52 rue Mirabeau, Deauville. Tel: 31.88.24.40.

Augusto, 27 rue Désiré-le-Hoc, Deauville. Tel: 31.88.34.49.

Restaurant de l'Aeroport, Deauville. Tel: 31.88.38.75.

Le Drakkar, 77 rue Eugène-Colas, Deauville. Tel: 31.88.71.24.

Hostellerie de Tourgéville, Tourgéville, nr Deauville. Tel: 31.88.63.40.

WHERE TO STAY ...

Hôtel Le Trophée, 81 rue du Général-Leclerc, Deauville. Tel: 31.88.45.86.

L'Augeval, 15 avenue Hocquart-de-Turtot, Deauville. Tel: 31.81.13.18.

Le Clos Saint-Gatien, Saint-Gatien-des-Bois, nr Deauville. Tel: 31.65.16.08.

L'Hostellerie de Tourgéville, Chemin de l'Orgueil, Tourgéville, nr Deauville. Tel: 31.88.63.40.

Trouville-sur-Mer

Slightly less glamorous than its illustrious neighbour Deauville, this resort is nonetheless popular, especially for its sandy beach. The riverside quays by La Touques offer a further attraction, as do the aquarium, art museum and exhibition gallery. The fish market, which is permanent, and the Sunday market, which specialises in regional produce, are both worth a browse round.

Following the coast northwards, you will get a fine view of Le Havre from Villerville. Don't miss the ivy-covered 11th century church at Criqueboeuf. Heading south a little, there are the remains of William the Conqueror's castle at Bonneville-sur-Touques. The view from the top of the tower is impressive.

WHERE TO GO FOR ...

GENERAL FARM PRODUCE
Les Producteurs Augerons, 79 rue Louvel et Brière, Touques, nr Trouville-sur-Mer. Tel: 31.98.06.60.

CALVADOS ETC.
Au P'tit Pointu, 22 rue des Bains, Trouville-sur-Mer. Tel: 31.98.36.20.

WHERE TO EAT ...

Les Roches Noires, 16 boulevard Louis-Bréguet, Trouville-sur-Mer. Tel: 31.88.12.19.

Les Vapeurs, 160 boulevard Fernand-Moureaux, Trouville-sur-Mer. Tel: 31.88.15.24.

Bistro du Port, 142 boulevard Fernand-Moureaux, Trouville-sur-Mer. Tel: 31.88.15.83.

Le Relais des Diligences, 7 rue du Dr Leneveu, Trouville-sur-Mer. Tel: 31.81.44.40.

Les Mouettes, 11 rue des Bains, Trouville-sur-Mer. Tel: 31.98.06.97.

Les Quatre Chats, 88 rue d'Orléans, Trouville-sur-Mer. Tel: 31.88.94.94.

La Petite Auberge, 7 rue Carnot, Trouville-sur-Mer. Tel: 31.88.11.07.

La Fée des Mers, 12 quai Batista-Monrival, Touques, nr Trouville-sur-Mer. Tel: 31.81.47.81.

WHERE TO STAY ...

Hôtel Carmen, 24 rue Carnot, Trouville-sur-Mer. Tel: 31.88.35.43.

Hôtel Le Central, 158 boulevard Fernand-Moureaux, Trouville-sur-Mer. Tel: 31.88.13.68.

Le Beach Hôtel, 1 quai Albert 1er, Trouville-sur-Mer. Tel: 31.98.12.00.

Le Saint-James, 16 rue de la Plage, Trouville-sur-Mer. Tel: 31.88.05.23.

Le Relais du Haras, 23 rue Louvel et Brière, Touques, nr Trouville-sur-Mer. Tel: 31.81.67.67.

Honfleur

This delightfully picturesque town is a model of architectural harmony and has, quite understandably, attracted artists and writers in search of inspiration. Once a key port for explorers crossing the Atlantic, the harbour is now full of colourful fishing boats which daily unload their catch. The intimate character of the small streets, alleyways and cafés makes Honfleur a popular spot for visitors to this corner of the Normandy coast. The old town is best represented by Place Hamelin, Rue Haute, Rue de l'Homme-de-Bois, Rue des Lingots and Rue du Puits. Try not to miss the Saturday morning market (for dairy produce, cheese and teurgoule, in particular) in Place Sainte-Catherine, where you can also see the fascinating 'wooden' church and belfry. You can visit the flower market on the same day in Place Arthur-Boudin.

The Old Dock (Vieux Bassin) with its Musée de la Marine, Musée d'Art Populaire (folk art) and the salt stores, Clocher and Eglise Sainte-Catherine, Musée Eugéne-Boudin (art) and, of course, Côte de Grâce. This peaceful hillside site above the town offers superb views across the Seine.

WHAT TO LOOK OUT FOR …

Prawns and shrimps. Also teurgoule and foie gras.

WHERE TO GO FOR …

FOIE GRAS
Jean Ouaknine, Haras de la Griserie, Genneville, nr Honfleur.
Tel: 31.98.74.52.

FRUIT & JAM
Alleaume Fruits, 84 rue Saint-Clair, La Rivière-Saint-Sauveur, nr Honfleur.
Tel: 31.89.04.48.

GLASS
Martial Mayel, 27 rue du Puits, Honfleur. Tel: 31.89.05.06.

WHERE TO EAT …

L'Assiette Gourmande, 2 quai des Passagers, Honfleur. Tel: 31.89.24.88.

Hostellerie Lechat, Place Sainte-Catherine, Honfleur. Tel: 31.89.23.85.

Le Champlain, 6 place Hamelin, Honfleur. Tel: 31.89.14.91.

Au Gars Normand, 8 quai des Passagers, Honfleur. Tel: 31.89.05.28.

Le P'tit Mareyeur, 4 rue Haute, Honfleur. Tel: 31.98.84.23.

Le Vieux Honfleur, 13 quai Saint-Etienne, Honfleur. Tel: 31.89.15.31.

L'Auberge de la Lieutenance, 12 place Sainte-Catherine, Honfleur. Tel: 31.89.07.52.

L'Auberge du Vieux Logis, Conteville, nr Honfleur. Tel: 32.57.60.16.

L'Eau Vive, Fatouville-Grestain, nr Honfleur. Tel: 32.57.67.44.

Le Chêne Pommier, Fatouville-Grestain, nr Honfleur. Tel: 32.57.61.42.

WHERE TO STAY …

Le Moderne, 20 quai Lepaulmier, Honfleur. Tel: 31.89.44.11.

L'Absinthe, 1 rue de la Ville, Honfleur. Tel: 31.89.39.00.

La Ferme Saint-Siméon, Rue Adolphe-Marais, Honfleur. Tel: 31.89.23.61.

Hôtel L'Ecrin, 19 rue Eugène-Boudin, Honfleur. Tel: 31.14.43.45.

La Chaumière, Vasouy, nr Honfleur. Tel: 31.81.63.20.

Pont-Audemer

Formerly a centre of the tanning industry, the town offers some pleasant views of the River Risle and some of its original character can be seen in the surviving 17th century half-timbered buildings – namely in Rue de la République, Impasse de l'Epée, Impasse Saint-Ouen and Cour Canel. Its two churches – Saint-Ouen and Saint-Germain – have 11th century origins, the former containing some exquisite stained-glass windows.

WHAT TO LOOK OUT FOR …

Rillettes made with rabbit, foie gras and *Mirliton*, a gâteau filled with chocolate and praline mousse. Also cheese, cider, calvados and *pommeau*.

RILLETTES
H Marcere, Boucherie-Charcuterie, 15/16 place du Général de Gaulle, Cormeilles, nr Pont-Audemer. Tel: 32.57.16.26.

FOIE GRAS
Franck Lavigne, Ferme de la Houssaye, Epaignes, nr Pont-Audemer. Tel: 32.42.53.53.

André Desvaux, Toutainville, nr Pont-Audemer. Also milk. Tel: 32.41.25.91.

CHEESE
Trehet, Fromager-Affineur, 7 rue Gambetta, Pont-Audemer. Tel: 32.41.04.98.

J-Jacques Patin, Pincheloup, Tourville, nr Pont-Audemer. Also dairy produce. Tel: 32.41.40.85.

CIDER ETC.
Hiblot-Lambert, Saint-Thurien, nr Pont-Audemer. Tel: 32.57.48.65.

Alain Daligaux, La Mare Bardin, Sainte-Opportune-la-Mare, nr Pont-Audemer. Tel: 32.42.47.00.

FRUIT & VEGETABLES
Aline Vadcard, La Hauquerie, Beuzeville, nr Pont-Audemer. Tel: 32.56.69.85.

Auberge de la Grande Mare, Place de l'Eglise, Sainte-Opportune-la-Mare, nr Pont-Audemer. Tel: 32.42.09.52.

L'Auberge du Vieux Puits, 6 rue Notre-Dame-du-Pré, Pont-Audemer. Tel: 32.41.01.48.

Belle-Isle-sur-Risle, 112 route de Rouen, Pont-Audemer. Tel: 32.56.96.22.

Le Drakkar, rue Georges Clémenceau, Pont-Audemer. Tel: 32.41.28.00.

Le Pilori, 38 place Victor Hugo, Pont-Audemer. Tel: 32.41.01.80.

Les Cloches de Corneville, Corneville-sur-Risle, nr Pont-Audemer. Tel: 32.57.01.04.

Le Petit Coq aux Champs, Campigny, nr Pont-Audemer. Tel: 32.41.04.19.

Le Relais de Poste, 60 rue Constant-Fouché, Beuzeville, nr Pont-Audemer. Tel: 32.57.71.04.

Routot

Cider, calvados and pommeau.

CIDER ETC.
M David, Calvados Rollon, Routot. Tel: 32.57.36.80.

François Bocquet, Château de la Boise, Epreville-en-Roumois, nr Routot. Tel: 32.56.26.40.

F Hue-Hermier, L'Aubrière, Bosgouet, nr Routot. Also goat's cheese and jam. Tel: 32.56.21.62.

Restaurant de Brotonne, Hauville, nr Routot. Tel: 32.57.34.11.

Auberge de l'Abbaye, Bourg-Achard, nr Routot. Tel: 32.57.07.29.

51

Lieurey

WHERE TO GO FOR ...

CHEESE
Domaine du Plessis, Noards, nr Lieurey.

DAIRY PRODUCE
Six Jean, Piencourt, nr Lieurey. Also poultry. Tel: 32.46.84.62.

FOIE GRAS
Franck Lavigne, La Houssaye, Epaignes, nr Lieurey. Also poultry. Tel: 32.42.53.53.

WHERE TO EAT ...

Ginette Esprit, Giverville, nr Lieurey. Must book. Tel: 32.45.96.69.

Le Pré Vert, Le Village Drucourt, Thiberville, nr Lieurey. Tel: 32.46.91.71.

Restaurant Le Pressoir, Carrefour La Bretagne, Le Favril, nr Lieurey. Tel: 32.45.94.22.

WHERE TO EAT & STAY ...

Le Commerce, 19 place Général-de-Gaulle, Cormeilles, nr Lieurey. Tel: 32.57.80.07.

Brionne

A medieval stronghold overlooking the Risle Valley, the town boasts an excellent example of a square Norman keep (11th century) – fine views from the top.

WHAT TO SEE ...

Le Donjon, Eglise Saint-Martin and Jardin de Shaftesbury. To the south-east is the 12th century Harcourt Château, with arboretum and forest. Travelling north, visit the abbey at Le Bec-Hellouin, an important medieval religious centre which provided two Archbishops of Canterbury – Lanfranc and Anselm. There is also a car museum. To the west lie the picturesque villages of Livet-sur-Authou and Saint-Benoît-des-Ombres, and Launay Château.

WHERE TO GO FOR ...

CIDER
E Join-Lambert, Domaine de la Houssaye, Brétigny, nr Brionne. Tel: 32.44.87.75.

FOIE GRAS
Jocelyne Garnier, La Croix Blanche, Livet-sur-Authou, nr Brionne. Tel: 32.45.70.41.

Alain Lercier, Route de Saint-Paul, Saint-Eloi-de-Fourques, nr Brionne. Also poultry. Tel: 32.35.30.43.

MUSHROOMS
Joël Coulon, La Briquetterie, Brionne. Tel: 32.44.26.27.

SNAILS
Pierre Fenoll, Les Pâtures, Bosrobert, nr Brionne. Tel: 32.45.76.31.

Jean-Yves Petit, 2 rue du Bouquet, Calleville, nr Brionne. Tel: 32.45.76.32.

WHERE TO EAT ...

Restaurant de la Tour, Place Guillaume le Conquérant, Le Bec Hellouin, nr Brionne. Tel: 32.44.86.15.

Auberge du Château, Harcourt, nr Brionne. Tel: 32.45.02.29.

WHERE TO EAT & STAY ...

L'Auberge de l'Abbaye, Le Bec Hellouin, nr Brionne. Tel: 32.44.86.02.

Le Logis de Brionne, 1 place Saint-Denis, Brionne. Tel: 32.44.81.73.

Le Soleil d'Or, La Rivière-Thibouville, nr Brionne. Tel: 32.55.00.08.

This is the main town of what is locally known as the 'Neubourg Plain'. A feature of the area is the great number of pretty churches with the inevitable yew tree. Le Neubourg is no exception. Its own example dates from the 16th century.

Foie gras. Special markets for foie gras from the end of October to mid-December.

FOIE GRAS
Lucien Michel, Marbeuf,
nr Le Neubourg. Tel: 32.35.86.36.

Paulette Demaegdt, Domaine de la Coudraye, La Haye-du-Theil, nr Le Neubourg. Also poultry.
Tel: 32.35.52.07.

POULTRY
Jean-Luc Braux, 7 rue Frimechon, Thibouville, nr Le Neubourg.
Tel: 32.43.42.19.

Côté Jardin, 10 rue du Docteur Couderc, Le Neubourg.
Tel: 32.85.81.89.

Auberge au Vieux Brabant, Le Gros Theil, nr Le Neubourg. Tel: 32.35.51.31.

The most impressive features of this small town are the ruins of the 13th century priory, with its heavy buttresses, and the restored 14th century church.

Cider, calvados and pommeau. Also foie gras.

CIDER ETC.
Jacques Serre, Goupillières, nr Beaumont-le-Roger. Tel: 32.45.10.14.

René Lesur, La Godinière, Le Noyer-en-Ouche, nr Beaumont-le-Roger.
Tel: 32.44.46.71.

Michel Parent, Saint-Aubin-le-Guichard, nr Beaumont-le-Roger. Tel: 32.44.41.04.

FOIE GRAS
Jean-Bernard Juin, Romilly-la-Puthenaye, nr Beaumont-le-Roger.
Tel: 32.30.22.28.

GOAT'S CHEESE
C Dorgere-Fauche, Le Chatelier, Le Noyer-en-Ouche, nr Beaumont-le-Roger. Tel: 32.30.70.49.

L'Etape Louis XIII, 2 route de la Barre-en-Ouche, Beaumesnil, nr Beaumont-le-Roger. Tel: 32.44.44.72.

Hostellerie du Lion-d'Or, 91 rue Saint-Nicholas, Beaumont-le-Roger.
Tel: 32.45.48.08.

Tucked into the Charentonne Valley, the town has some interesting half-timbered buildings and a 17th century Hôtel de Ville (town hall). You will get a fine view of both Bernay and the valley from Le Boulevard des Monts. L'Ancienne Eglise Abbatiale is all that remains of an 11th century abbey.

WHAT TO SEE ...

Ancienne Eglise Abbatiale, Eglise Sainte-Croix, Basilique Notre-Dame-de-la-Couture, Hôtel de Ville, Musée Municipale and Rue Gaston-Follope – full of antique dealers. To the south-east is the splendid Beaumesnil Château, built in the Louis XIII style.

WHAT TO LOOK OUT FOR ...

Trout, cider, calvados and pommeau. Show in mid-March. Also special market for foie gras in mid-June.

WHERE TO GO FOR ...

CHARCUTERIE ETC.
Eric Lamboy, Charcutier-Traiteur, Au Cochon d'Or, 50 rue Thiers, Bernay. Tel: 32.43.14.59.

FOIE GRAS
Jean-Noël Montier, Le Mesnil, Sainte-Marguerite-en-Ouche, nr Bernay. Tel: 32.44.46.85.

Patrick Laforse, La Trinité-de-Réville, nr Bernay. Tel: 32.44.27.17.

Philippe Lemaire, Le Val Fleuri, Drucourt, nr Bernay. Tel: 32.46.85.83.

J-F Rabier, La Valaiserie, Saint-Germain-la-Campagne, nr Bernay. Tel: 32.44.89.00.

CALVADOS
Pierre Dubus, Le Coudray, Courbépine, nr Bernay. Tel: 32.43.20.19.

CIDER ETC.
Etienne Plet, La Bretterie, Carsix, nr Bernay. Tel: 32.46.16.25.

SNAILS
Nadia Decock, Le Bellou, Landepereuse, nr Bernay. Tel: 32.44.39.49.

WHERE TO EAT ...

La Vieille Auberge, Le Mesnil de Courbépine, nr Bernay. Tel: 32.43.19.00.

La Pommeraie, N138, Saint-Quentin-des-Isles, nr Bernay. Tel: 32.45.28.88.

Le Moulin Fouret, Saint-Aubin-le-Vertueux, nr Bernay. Tel: 32.43.19.95.

WHERE TO EAT & STAY ...

L'Acropole, N138, Bernay. Tel: 32.45.18.18.

This small town boasts some delightful half-timbered buildings (Grande Rue), an enormous tower beside the church (Notre-Dame) and the 16th century Vieux Manoir, now housing the municipal museum. Just to the south you can trace the source of the River Orbiquet which flows through Orbec.

WHERE TO GO FOR ...

TROUT
Daufresne et Fils, La Cressonnière, nr Orbec-en-Auge. Tel: 31.62.11.59.

L'Orbecquoise, 60 Grande Rue, Orbec-en-Auge. Tel: 31.62.44.99.

Au Caneton, Orbec-en-Auge. Tel: 31.32.73.32.

Lisieux

This busy town in the Auge region is dominated by the enormous basilica, perched on the top of a hill. It was consecrated in 1954 and dedicated to the local Sainte Thérèse. You can visit the house (Les Buissonnets) where she lived as a child, which has much of interest to offer. There is also a 12th century cathedral.

WHAT TO SEE ...

Basilique Sainte-Thérèse, Cathédrale Saint-Pierre, Palais de Justice and Musée du Vieux Lisieux. Just to the north, Ouilly-le-Vicomte boasts one of Normandy's oldest churches – dating from the 10th century. Due south, there is a curious but strikingly elegant château at Saint-Germain-de-Livet – a combination of chequered stone and brick with adjoining half-timber of 15th century origin. The inside is equally impressive.

WHAT TO LOOK.OUT FOR ...

Vallée d'Auge chicken, foie gras, cuisine à la crème, Pont-l'Evêque cheese, cider, calvados, pommeau.

WHERE TO GO FOR ...

CHEESE
Pierre Levasseur, Fromageries Paul-Renard, Saint-Désir-de-Lisieux, Lisieux.

CIDER ETC.
Distillerie du Houley, Ouilly-du-Houley, nr Lisieux. Tel: 31.63.63.46.

Léon Desfrieches, Route de Dives, Saint-Désir-de-Lisieux, nr Lisieux. Tel: 31.61.14.57.

François David, Blangy-le-Château, nr Lisieux. Tel: 31.64.76.66.

Distillerie du Moulin de la Foulonnerie, Coquainvilliers, nr Lisieux.

Philippe Daufresne, Le Mont Hélery, Ouilly-le-Vicomte, nr Lisieux. Tel: 31.62.29.84.

B Charbonneau, Ferme des Bruyères, Moyaux, nr Lisieux. Tel: 31.62.81.98.

SMOKED FISH ETC.
Au Saumon Bleu, Chemin de Mesnil Asselin, Lisieux. Tel: 31.31.39.62.

FOIE GRAS
André Geldy, Le Mesnil-Eudes, nr Lisieux. Tel: 31.61.07.79.

POTTERY
Jacques Thomasse, 100 bis boulevard Herbet Fournet, Lisieux. Tel: 31.62.25.39.

PAINTED WOOD
Mecki Dauré, Le Cotil, Route de Falaise, Le Mesnil-Simon, nr Lisieux. Tel: 31.31.47.86.

TANNING
Jean-Claude Blanche, Le Pont de Glos, Glos, nr Lisieux. Tel: 31.62.75.29.

WHERE TO EAT ...

L'Oxer, Boulevard Sainte-Anne, Lisieux. Tel: 31.62.04.76.

WHERE TO EAT & STAY ...

Hotel de la Place, 67 rue Henry Chéron, Lisieux. Tel: 31.31.17.44.

Garden's, N13, Lisieux. Tel: 31.61.17.17.

Pont-l'Evêque

Although buildings suffered in the last war, the town's renown for its fine cheese did survive – along with a handful of old houses, mainly in Rue Saint-Michel and Rue de Vaucelles. The church (Saint-Michel) is impressive, as are its modern stained-glass windows. Other places of note include the half-timbered old convent next to the Tribunal, Hôtel Montpensier and Hôtel Brilly – now the town hall and tourist office.

WHAT TO SEE ...

Musée du Calvados et des Métiers Anciens in Route de Trouville. To the north-west, you will find the charming 13th century Manoir des Evêques de Lisieux at Canapville.

WHAT TO LOOK OUT FOR ...

Pont-l'Evêque cheese, which was first made in the 13th century. Show at the beginning of May. Also goat, dairy produce, calvados, pommeau and cider.

WHERE TO GO FOR ...

TARTES & BRIOCHES
Michel Thomas, Boulangerie-Patisserie des Dominicaines, 61 rue Saint-Michel, Pont-l'Evêque. Tel: 31.64.04.08.

CALVADOS ETC.
Fiefs Sainte-Anne, N177, Coudray-Rabut, nr Pont-l'Evêque. Tel: 31.98.80.16.

Château du Breuil, Le Breuil-en-Auge, nr Pont-l'Evêque. Tel: 31.65.07.76.

Jules Hommet, La Ferme Sainte-Marie, Saint-Julian-sur-Calonne, nr Pont-l'Evêque. Also dairy produce. Tel: 31.64.08.26.

William Langin, La Vicomte d'Auge, Clarbec, nr Pont-l'Evêque. Also honey. Tel: 31.65.15.90.

CIDER
Michel Bréavoine, La Ferme du Lieu Gosset, Route de Honfleur, Coudray-Rabut, nr Pont-l'Evêque. Tel: 31.64.06.57.

M & Mme Michel Boissel, Saint-André-d'Hébertot, nr Pont-l'Evêque. Also rooms. Tel: 31.65.40.79.

GOAT
Le Fresnay, Saint Hymer, nr Pont-l'Evêque. Tel: 31.64.15.95.

ALL FARM PRODUCE
Les Agriculteurs de la Côte Fleurie, Annebault, nr Pont-l'Evêque. Tel: 31.64.82.16.

WHERE TO EAT ...

L'Auberge de l'Aigle d'Or, 68 rue de Vaucelles, Pont-l'Evêque. Tel: 31.65.05.25.

L' Auberge des Deux Tonneaux, Route des Douets, D48, Pierrefitte-en-Auge, nr Pont-l'Evêque. Tel: 31.64.09.31.

L' Auberge de l'Abbaye, 1 rue de la Libération, Beaumont-en-Auge, nr Pont-l'Evêque. Tel: 31.64.82.31.

Le Dauphin, Le Breuil-en-Auge, nr Pont-l'Evêque. Tel: 31.65.08.11.

Le Vert Buisson, Saint-Gatien-des-Bois, nr Pont-l'Evêque. Tel: 31.65.16.62.

Le Manoir de Roncheville, Saint-Martin-aux-Chartrins, nr Pont-l'Evêque. Tel: 31.65.14.14.

WHERE TO STAY & EAT ...

Hôtel Climat, Centre de Loisirs, Pont-l'Evêque. Tel: 31.64.64.00.

Le Cardinal, Carrefour d'Annebault, Annebault, nr Pont-l'Evêque. Tel: 31.64.81.96.

Auberge du Prieuré, Saint-André-d'Hébertot, nr Pont-l'Evêque. Tel: 31.64.03.03.

Le Clos Saint-Gatien, Saint-Gatien-des-Bois, nr Pont-l'Evêque. Tel: 31.65.16.08.

Camembert Country

This tour, which begins from Ouistreham, is certainly one for the gourmet, since it includes some of the best 'cheese country' in Normandy. Camembert and Livarot are the principal stopping-off points on your way round. And you will certainly not have any trouble finding places to sample the local cider and its various derivatives. You continue your journey south to Argentan, famous for its lace, before heading back via Falaise – almost medieval in its rugged valley setting – to Caen, the proud capital of Basse Normandie.

YOUR ROUTE ...

D514 from Ouistreham to Cabourg & Dives-sur-Mer.

D49 to Beuvron-en-Auge.

D146 then D85 to Forges, Rumesnil & Cambremer.

D101 to Saint-Loup-de-Fribois.

D16 to Saint-Pierre-sur-Dives.

D4 to Livarot.

D579 to Vimoutiers.

(D246 to Camembert)

D979 to Gacé.

D14 then N26 to Argentan.

N158 to Falaise & Caen.

See map overleaf.

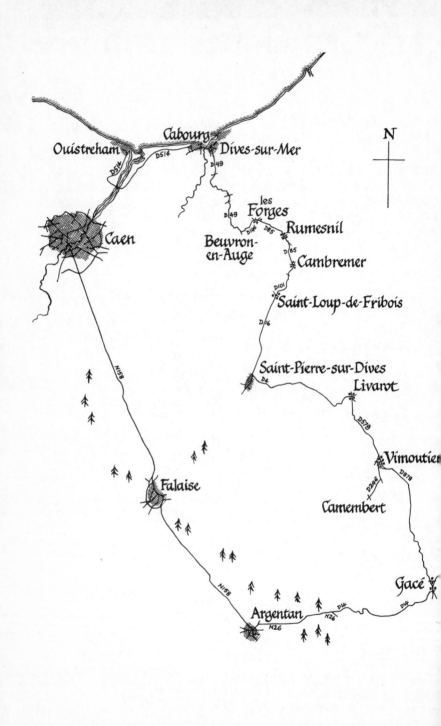

This delightful little village with charming timber-framed houses round the former market square also has an intriguing manor house with ornate wood carvings.

WHAT TO LOOK OUT FOR ...

Pavé d'Auge cheese, cuisine *à la crème*, cider, calvados and *pommeau*.

WHERE TO GO FOR ...

CIDER ETC.
Ferme Saint-Gilles, Rumesnil, nr Beuvron-en-Auge. Tel: 31.63.03.18.

CALVADOS
Denise David, Manoir de Sens, Beuvron-en-Auge. Tel: 31.79.23.05.

ALL PRODUCE
La Ferme de Beuvron, Le Bourg, Beuvron-en-Auge. Tel: 31.79.29.19.

POTTERY
Atelier de Brocottes, Hotot-en-Auge, nr Beuvron-en-Auge.

WHERE TO EAT ...

Le Pavé d'Auge, Beuvron-en-Auge. Tel: 31.79.26.71.

Le Café de la Forge, Beuvron-en-Auge.

Chez Michel, Putot-en-Auge, nr Beuvron-en-Auge. Tel: 31.79.20.29.

Le Laizon, Cléville, nr Beuvron-en-Auge. Must book. Tel: 31.23.64.67.

WHERE TO STAY ...

Cour L'Epée, Saint-Aubin-Lébizay, nr Beuvron-en-Auge. Tel: 31.65.09.45.

Le Haras de Bouttemont, Victot-Pontfol, nr Beuvron-en-Auge. Tel: 31.63.00.41.

Cambremer

Make a point of coming here at Easter or in July or August, when Cambremer turns back the clock with its traditional markets (Sunday mornings), and the local producers and artisans dress up in costume. Among a number of châteaux that lie in the district surrounding this village, the most impressive is that of Crèvecoeur to the south. Recently restored, the original fortified half-timbered buildings were altered in the 15th century. With moats and trees around it, the whole site is very picturesque. Make sure to see the fascinating dovecot. There is also a 12th century chapel and the Schlumberger Museum.

WHAT TO LOOK OUT FOR ...

Cider, calvados, pommeau and *poiré*. Each year the very finest producers of cider and calvados in the area receive the 'Cru de Cambremer' award. There are a couple of dozen (at least) in the villages around – too numerous to list here. Look for the signs. Also goat's cheese.

CHEESE
Jacques Antoine Motte, Cambremer.
Tel: 31.63.00.50.

L'Auberge de la Route du Cidre,
Montreuil-en-Auge, nr Cambremer.

Château Les Bruyères, Route du
Cadran, Cambremer. Tel: 31.63.78.30.

Saint-Loup-de-Fribois

Calvados, cider and pommeau.
Also camembert cheese and dairy
produce.

CIDER ETC.
Pierre Rosset, La Prieuré, Saint-Loup-
de-Fribois. Also rooms. Tel: 31.63.02.09.

André Vilain, Crèvecoeur, nr Saint-
Loup-de-Fribois. Tel: 31.63.03.83.

Daniel Requier, Le Lieu Fergan,
Monteille, nr Saint-Loup-de-Fribois.
Tel: 31.63.04.29.

CHEESE
Le Domaine de Saint-Loup, Saint-
Loup-de-Fribois. Tel: 31.63.04.04.

DAIRY PRODUCE
J-Marie Gasson, Les Patis, Méry-Corbon,
nr Saint-Loup-de-Fribois. Especially
confiture du lait. Tel: 31.23.66.21.

Les Pommiers, Notre-Dame-de-Livaye,
nr Saint-Loup-de-Fribois. Must book.
Tel: 31.63.01.28.

Au Repos des Chineurs, Chemin de
l'Eglise, Notre-Dame-d'Estrées, nr Saint-
Loup-de-Fribois. Tel: 31.63.72.51.

Saint-Pierre-sur-Dives

Formerly the site of a rich Benedictine abbey, of which the
church still remains, this small
town provides most of the boxes in
which the cheeses of Normandy
are packaged. A museum showing
the techniques of cheese-making is
housed in another part of the old
abbey. Although the 12th century
covered market (Les Halles) suffered greatly in the last war, it has
been lovingly restored to its past
glory. Make sure you visit it on a
Monday to catch all the local produce. On the first Sunday of each
month, there is an antiques market.
To the south-west, Vendeuvre
provides a fine example of a lived-
in château. There is also a water
garden and an impressive collection of miniature furniture in the
museum.

Cheese, dairy produce, foie gras,
poultry, cider, calvados and pommeau.

CHEESE
Michel Touze, Le Bocquet, Vieux-Pont-
en-Auge, nr Saint-Pierre-sur-Dives.
Tel: 31.20.78.67.

Laiteries de Bernières, Bernières-
d'Ailly, nr Saint-Pierre-sur-Dives.
Tel: 31.40.94.09.

Fromagerie Thébault, La Houssaye, Boissey, nr Saint-Pierre-sur-Dives. Tel: 31.20.64.00.

Musée des Techniques Fromagères, Rue Saint-Benoit, Saint-Pierre-sur-Dives. Tel: 31.20.97.90.

DAIRY PRODUCE
Laiterie du Moulin de Carel, Carel, nr Saint-Pierre-sur-Dives. Tel: 31.20.84.57.

Le Boquet, Vieux-Pont-en-Auge, nr Saint-Pierre-sur-Dives.

Au Frisson Normand, Ferme de la Houssaye, Garnetot, nr Saint-Pierre-sur-Dives. Also ice cream. Tel: 31.90.70.07.

ALL PRODUCE
Annick Vanhoutte, Le Bois Tilly, Vendeuvre, nr Saint-Pierre-sur-Dives. Tel: 31.40.91.87.

L'Auberge de la Levrette, Route de Lisieux, Saint-Julien-le-Faucon, nr Saint-Pierre-sur-Dives. Tel: 31.63.81.20.

Livarot

This is the home of yet another of Normandy's celebrated cheeses – also called 'colonel' – which is quite strong and has a distinctively orangey colour. There are some delightful old buildings in the town.

WHAT TO SEE ...

To the north-east, the massive stone and brick château overlooks the River Touques at Fervaques. Heading south-east, see the 16th century manor at Bellou and the Musée Fernand-Léger (commemorating that artist) at Lisores.

WHAT TO LOOK OUT FOR ...

Livarot cheese. Festival on the first weekend of August. Also dairy produce and cider, calvados and pommeau.

WHERE TO GO FOR ...

LIVAROT CHEESE
Fromagerie Thébault, Boissey, nr Livarot. Tel: 31.20.64.00.

E Graindorge, 42 rue Général Leclerc, Livarot. Tel: 31.63.50.02.

Musée du Fromage de Livarot, Manoir de l'Isle, 68 rue Marcel-Gambier, Livarot. Tel: 31.63.43.13.

PONT-L'EVÊQUE CHEESE
Didier Lallier, Ferme de la Moissonnière, Fervaques, nr Livarot. Tel: 31.32.31.23.

DAIRY PRODUCE
Marcel Julian, Le Mesnil-Germain, nr Livarot. Tel: 31.63.54.58.

CIDER ETC.
Cidreries du Calvados, Route de Lisieux, Livarot. Tel: 31.63.50.33.

Philippe Pinoir, Notre-Dame-de-Courson, nr Livarot. Tel: 31.32.30.15.

Marc de Lesdain, Sainte-Foy-de-Montgommery, nr Livarot. Tel: 31.63.53.07.

CALVADOS
Henriette Conan, Lisores, nr Livarot. Tel: 31.63.53.22.

ALL PRODUCE
Les Amis de Coupesarte, Coupesarte, nr Livarot. Tel: 31.63.82.84.

EMBROIDERY
Martine Fournier, Le Bourg, Saint-Georges-en-Auge, nr Livarot. Tel: 31.20.67.59.

MARQUETRY
Sylvie de Neuville, L'Angleterre, Livarot. Tel: 31.63.40.30.

Le Cottage, Route de Lisieux,
Livarot. Tel: 31.32.04.10.

Hôtel de Normandie, 12 rue de
Lisieux, Livarot. Tel: 31.63.52.36.

Vimoutiers

This little town, set in a valley and surrounded by cider orchards, also boasts of being the 'City of Camembert'. There is a statue in memory of the cheese's founder – Marie Harel – in the main square and a fascinating museum showing its history and manufacture.

WHAT TO SEE ...

To the south, the tiny village of Camembert (see below) where it all started. To the west, the priory (Saint-Michel) at Crouttes with a 13th century tithe barn, ancient apple press and the traditional vegetable and herb gardens.

WHAT TO LOOK OUT FOR ...

Camembert cheese, cider, calvados, pommeau, *tarte aux pommes*, farm butter and Normandy beef. Also foie gras! Gastronomical events include La Foire de Pâques (Easter) for cider, calvados and pommeau (the oldest and best-known in Normandy), an international show for *tarte aux pommes* and La Foire de la Pomme in October.

WHERE TO GO FOR ...

CALVADOS ETC.
Claude & Jean-Luc Olivier, La
Galotière, Crouttes, nr Vimoutiers.
Tel: 33.39.05.98.

Etablissements Anée, 27 rue du
Perré, Vimoutiers. Tel: 33.39.00.00.

Jean-Pierre & Annie Gautard,
Le Vaucanu, Saint-Germain-de-
Montgommery, nr Vimoutiers. Also
rooms. Tel: 33.39.25.13.

Jean-Pierre Pinot, Le Beau-Levesque,
Canapville, nr Vimoutiers. Also butter &
cream. Tel: 33.39.11.97.

CIDER
Régis Liard, La Croix Blanche,
Vimoutiers. Tel: 33.39.32.05.

CHEESE
H & R Barbot, GAEC de la Forêt de
Survie, Survie, nr Vimoutiers.
Tel: 33.39.95.72.

Musée du Camembert, 10 avenue du
Général de Gaulle, Vimoutiers.
Tel: 33.39.30.29.

FOIE GRAS
Monique de Carne, Hameau des
Vesques, Canapville, nr Vimoutiers.
Tel: 33.39.12.96.

TROUT
Ginette Deshayes, La Fauvetière,
Vimoutiers. Tel: 33.39.15.99.

WHERE TO EAT ...

Les Bruyères, Les Champeaux-en-
Auge, nr Vimoutiers. Tel: 33.39.11.81.

Daniel Guidez, Elevage du Haut-de-
Crouttes, Crouttes, nr Vimoutiers. Must
book. Tel: 33.35.25.27.

WHERE TO STAY ...

La Chasterie, Route de Vimoutiers,
Mardilly, nr Vimoutiers.
Tel: 33.35.73.42.

L'Escale du Vitou, D916, Le Vitou, nr
Vimoutiers. Tel: 33.39.12.04.

Camembert

The home of the world-famous cheese, first made two centuries ago by Marie Harel in this tiny village. You can still see the traditional method of production in some of the farms around.

WHAT TO LOOK OUT FOR ...

Camembert cheese and dairy produce.

WHERE TO GO FOR ...

CHEESE
François Durand, Ferme de la Heronnière, Camembert. Tel: 33.39.08.08.

DAIRY PRODUCE
GAEC Goupil, La Heurtaudière, Camembert. Tel: 33.39.10.75.

Gacé

This small town lies on the edge of the Forêt de Saint-Evroult, with some delightful riverside scenery to the north and south along the banks of the Touques river.

WHAT TO SEE ...

To the east, the abbey at Saint-Evroult-Notre-Dame – founded in the 6th century, rebuilt at various stages but now in ruins – with a museum showing the monks' work. To the west, Exmes – a former capital of the region – and the nearby 15th century manor at Argentelles. The church at Saint-Germain-de-Clairfeuille, to the south-west, contains some marvellous wooden panelling.

WHAT TO LOOK OUT FOR ...

Cider, calvados and pommeau.

Also foie gras, cheese and dairy produce. There is a special market for foie gras at the beginning of December.

WHERE TO GO FOR ...

CIDER ETC.
Michel Hubert, Les Vergers de la Morinière, La Fresnaie-Fayel, nr Gacé. Tel: 33.35.51.13.

CALVADOS
Maurice Bouvry, Le Pont, Mardilly, nr Gacé. Tel: 33.35.60.10.

FOIE GRAS
Claude Guillotin, La Chantereine, Avernes-sous-Exmes, nr Gacé. Tel: 33.36.19.88.

CHEESE & DAIRY PRODUCE
M & Mme Droulin, GAEC des Courgentils, La Mercerie, Saint-Evroult-de-Monfort, nr Gacé. Tel: 33.36.55.43.

Argentan

This ancient town is set on the hillside overlooking the confluence of the Orne and Ure rivers in what is mainly cattle-rearing country. A familiar touch of history is associated with the place – once in English hands – since it was from here that some of Henry II's knights set out to murder Thomas à Becket in Canterbury Cathedral. And it was from this area that the final thrust came in the Battle of Normandy in August 1944. Also another centre of the old lace industry.

WHAT TO SEE ...

Eglise Saint-Germain, Chapelle Saint-Nicholas, Eglise Saint-Martin and the Abbaye des Bénédictines, where you can see examples of the famous Argentan lace stitch. Also, to the south, the 18th century Château Sassy and the church at Saint-Christophe-le-Jajolet, an old point of pilgrimage to the patron saint of travellers. To the west, the village of Ecouché, still 'protected' by a lone French tank and with an interesting unfinished church dating back to the 13th century. To the east, Haras-du-Pin – one of France's most celebrated horse-breeding centres in a magnificent woodland setting.

WHAT TO LOOK OUT FOR ...

Daguet, young stag of 15-27 months, which is reared, killed and prepared locally. Show in October. Also cider, calvados, pommeau and poiré.

WHERE TO GO FOR ...

DEER PARK
Alain de Quenetain, Domaine de la Bonnerie, Sevigny, Argentan.
Tel: 33.36.50.11.

CIDER ETC.
Gérard Perigault, Silly-en-Gouffern, nr Argentan. Tel: 33.67.11.85.

CALVADOS
Michel Leplat, La Touche, Montabard, nr Argentan. Tel: 33.35.91.69.

POULTRY
Patrick Besnouin, Earl de l'Epinette, Le Marais, Urou, nr Argentan.
Tel: 33.36.13.09.

TROUT
Alain Langlois, Pisciculture Artisanale Moulin-Neuf, Nécy, nr Argentan.
Tel: 33.35.94.23.

Pisciculture Occagnes, Le Bail H, Occagnes, nr Argentan. Tel: 33.67.33.63.

WHERE TO EAT ...

L'Auberge de l'Ancienne Abbaye, 25 rue Saint-Martin, Argentan.
Tel: 33.39.37.42.

La Renaissance, 20 avenue de la 2ème D B, Argentan. Tel: 33.36.14.20.

Clérembaux, D2, Fleuré, nr Argentan. Tel: 33.36.10.85.

WHERE TO EAT & STAY ...

Le Faisan Doré, Fontenai-sur-Orne, nr Argentan. Tel: 33.67.18.11.

Le Pavillon de Gouffern, Silly-en-Gouffern, nr Argentan. Tel: 33.36.64.26.

The birthplace of William the Conqueror, this small town in the rocky setting of the Ante Valley is dominated by its medieval fortress. It is particularly notable for two 12th century keeps and the 35-metre high Tour de Talbot. Other interesting sights include its three churches, a delightful stone gateway (part of the old walls) and a fountain in memory of William's mother Arlette. Falaise is an ideal centre from which to tour Suisse Normande.

WHAT TO SEE ...

The castle, Eglise de la Trinité, Eglise Saint-Gervais, Eglise Notre-Dame-de-Guibray, Porte des Cordeliers and Fontaine d'Arlette. To the north, at Soumont-Saint-Quentin, there is an interesting little museum depicting rural life in Basse Normandie.

WHAT TO LOOK OUT FOR ...

Crepinettes, long sausages and smoked garlic sausage. Shows in spring and autumn. Also foie gras, honey, calvados, cider, pommeau and poiré.

WHERE TO GO FOR ...

Brioche, chocolates & ice cream
Martin, Maître Artisan Pâtissier, Pont-d'Ouilly, nr Falaise. Tel: 31.69.39.54.

CALVADOS ETC.
Cidrerie-Distillerie Chapron, Martigny-sur-l'Ante, nr Falaise. Tel: 31.40.70.02.

Lemonnier, Ferme de Saint-Quentin, Soumont-Saint-Quentin, nr Falaise. Tel: 31.90.88.18.

Claude Courvallet, Les Vergers de Plainville, Pierrefitte-en-Cinglais, nr Falaise. Tel: 31.40.70.81.

FOIE GRAS
Mme Colette Leneveu, Le Hameau, Villy-lez-Falaise, nr Falaise. Tel: 31.90.76.54.

GAEC des Massinots, Saint-Germain-le-Vasson, nr Falaise. Tel: 31.90.56.54.

HONEY & ROYAL JELLY
H Marie, Cordey, nr Falaise. Tel: 31.90.27.69.

WHERE TO EAT ...

Les Massinots, Saint-Germain-le-Vasson, nr Falaise. Must book. Tel: 31.90.54.22.

Domaine de Torps, Villers-Canivet, nr Falaise. Must book. Tel: 31.90.82.52.

WHERE TO EAT & STAY ...

Hôtel de la Poste, 38 rue Georges-Clémenceau, Falaise. Tel: 31.90.13.14.

Château du Tertre, Saint-Martin-de-Mieux, nr Falaise. Tel: 31.90.01.04.

This is the capital of Basse Normandie, and it has now been dramatically restored and greatly developed after the bombings in the summer of 1944 reduced much of it to rubble. The centre is dominated by its castle, whose origins date back to William the Conqueror. Sited on a mound, its massive walls have been rebuilt following severe war damage. Inside are housed two museums – Beaux-Arts and Normandie. Below stands the equally impressive Eglise Saint-Pierre, begun in the 13th century and completed in the 16th century. Other important landmarks include L'Abbaye aux Hommes with the adjoining Eglise Saint-Etienne, and L'Abbaye aux Dames with L'Eglise de la Trinité. The marina – Le Bassin Saint-Pierre – enables yachts and other leisure craft to moor in the very centre of the town. The port was originally served by the River Orne, but the canal from Ouistreham – built in the middle of the 19th century – has enabled the extensive dockland to flourish. One of the most significant sights is The Memorial, on the north-east side of the town, which represents a 'Museum for Peace'. Here you can witness the most important events of the 20th century with the help of modern-day audio-visual and computer techniques. For local produce, the best market is on Fridays at Place Saint-Sauveur.

WHAT TO SEE ...

The Memorial, Château, Eglise Saint-Pierre, Abbaye aux Hommes, Abbaye aux Dames, Eglise Saint-Saveur, Hôtel d'Escoville, Rue Saint-Pierre, Musée de la Poste et des Techniques de Communication, Rue du Vaugueux and Jardin des Plantes. To the north-west, there is the curious little Romanesque church at Thaon and the superb Renaissance château at Fontaine-Henry, built on the site of an 11th century fortress. Just to the west is l'Abbaye d'Ardenne and to the south, Fontaine-Etoupefour Château, complete with moat and drawbridge.

WHAT TO LOOK OUT FOR ...

Tripe à la mode de Caen, for which there is an annual international show. Also calvados, cider, pommeau and apple juice. Special festival for foie gras at the end of September. Also chocolates, caramels (chiques) and boiled sweets (berlingots).

WHERE TO GO FOR ...

TRIPE
Daniel Marie, Boucher-Charcutier, 30-32 avenue du Calvados, Caen. Tel: 31.94.44.55.

Bernard Noêl, Charcutier, 119 rue Saint-Jean, Caen. Tel: 31.86.21.60.

L Amaglio, Charcutier, 23 place du Commerce, Grace de Dieu, Caen. Tel: 31.52.18.13.

R Le Fourkié, Charcutier-Traiteur, 42 rue Chapron, Mondeville, nr Caen. Tel: 31.52.13.80.

FOIE GRAS
Les Fermiers du Bec, 6 promenade Mme de Sévigné, Caen. Tel: 31.70.25.73.

CALVADOS ETC
Henri Vaucrecy, 31 rue de l'Eglise, Rots, nr Caen. Tel: 31.26.50.51.

Les Caves Thorel, 32 rue Neuve-Saint-Jean, Caen. Tel: 31.86.07.46.

CHEESE
Crémerie du 6 Juin, 6 avenue du 6 Juin, Caen. Tel: 31.85.45.03.

Aux Fromages de France, 116 rue Saint-Jean, Caen. Tel: 31.86.14.53.

CHOCOLATES
Témoins, 69 rue Saint-Pierre, Caen. Tel: 31.86.31.88.

Hotot, 13 rue Saint-Pierre, Caen. Tel: 31.86.31.90.

FRUIT & JAM
Bruno Fremont, Roncheville, Bavent, nr Caen. Tel: 31.78.84.22.

POTTERY
Tuilerie Normande, Bavent, nr Caen. Tel: 31.78.80.10.

COPPER & PEWTER
Cuivres et Etains de Sannerville, ZA de Lizore, Sannerville, nr Caen. Tel: 31.23.30.51.

WHERE TO EAT ...

La Bourride, 15 rue du Vaugueux, Caen. Tel: 31.93.29.63.

L'Alcide, Place Courtonne, Caen. Tel: 31.44.18.06.

Le Carlotta, 16 quai Vendeuvre, Caen. Tel: 31.86.68.99.

Le Paquebot, 7 rue des Croisiers, Caen. Tel: 31.85.10.10.

La Bon'iau, 8 quai de l'Amiral Hamelin, Caen. Tel: 31.82.26.55.

Le Rabelais, Place Foch, Caen. Tel: 31.27.57.56.

Daniel Tuboeuf, 8 rue Buquet, Caen. Tel: 31.43.64.48.

Le Laëtitia, Sainte-Honorine-la-Chardonnerette, Herouvillette, nr Caen. Tel: 31.72.40.57.

La Valise Gourmande, 7 route de Lion-sur-Mer, Cresserons, nr Caen. Tel: 31.37.39.10.

L'Auberge Les Peupliers, 25 route de Rouen, Giberville, nr Caen. Tel: 31.72.36.53.

Le Relais de Lorguichon, N158, Rocquancourt, nr Caen. Tel: 31.79.82.51.

Les Aucrais, Cauvicourt, nr Caen. Tel: 31.78.06.16.

Hostellerie du Moulin du Pré, D95, Bavent, nr Caen. Tel: 31.78.83.68.

WHERE TO EAT & STAY ...

Relais des Gourmets (L), 15 rue de Geôle, Caen. Tel: 31.86.06.01.

Le Dauphin (L), 29 rue Gémare, Caen. Tel: 31.86.22.26.

Hôtel Mercure (L), Place Courtonne, Caen. Tel: 31.47.24.24.

Holiday Inn (M), Place Foch, Caen. Tel: 31.27.57.57.

La Grande Bruyère (M), D37, Touffréville, nr Caen. Tel: 31.23.32.74.

WHERE TO STAY ...

Les Cordeliers (M), 4 rue des Cordeliers, Caen. Tel: 31.86.37.15.

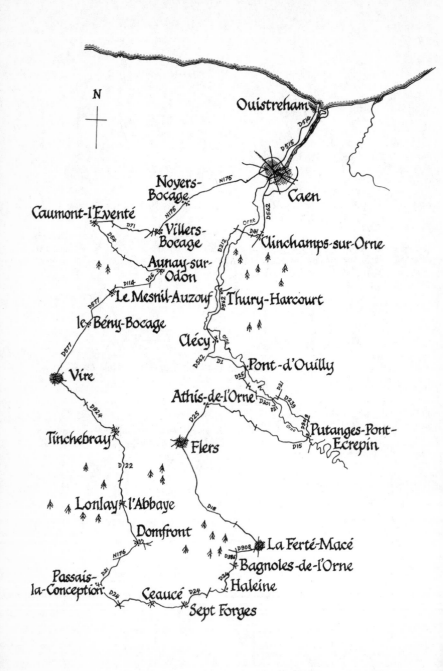

Suisse Normande

This tour, which begins at Caen (see above), takes you through some of the most delightful – and at times spectacular – country in the whole of Normandy. It is the ideal route for those who want to get out of their cars and walk. The area's main feature is the route of the River Orne, as it wends its way through steep wooded banks and ancient rocks, from the top of which panoramic views await the more energetic. The area round Domfront is the ideal place to find *poiré*, while at Vire the celebrated *andouille* awaits. Then it is on through the *bocage* – a countryside almost lost in woodland and well worth exploring as you make your way back to Caen.

YOUR ROUTE ...

D514 then D515 from Ouistreham to Caen.

D562 then D41 to Clinchamps-sur-Orne.

D41 then D212 to Thury-Harcourt.

D562 to Clécy.

D562 then D1 to Pont-d'Ouilly.

D25, D301, D21, D239 then D909 to Putanges-Pont-Ecrepin.

D15 to Athis-de-l'Orne.

D25 to Flers.

D18 to La Ferté-Macé.

D908 then D386 to Bagnoles-de-l'Orne.

D24 to Haleine, Sept Forges, Ceaucé & Passais-la-Conception.

D21 then N176 to Domfront.

D22 to Lonlay-l'Abbé & Tinchebray.

D924 to Vire.

D577 to Beny-Bocage & Le Mesnil-Auzouf.

D114 then D26 to Aunay-sur-Odon.

D54 to Caumont-l'Eventé.

D71 to Villers-Bocage.

N175 to Noyers-Bocage & Caen.

Clinchamps-sur-Orne

Brasillé, a dessert made with pure butter. Also tripe, poultry and rabbits.

BRASILLÉ
Emile & Bruno Roussel, Brasillé de Clinchamps, Clinchamps-sur-Orne. Tel: 31.79.82.22. Also at Fleury-sur-Orne. Tel: 31.78.26.09.

TRIPE
Boucheries Plumail, Urville, nr Clinchamps-sur-Orne. Tel: 31.23.52.71.

POULTRY ETC.
Didier Levasseur, 4 rue des Fosses, Evrecy, nr Clinchamps-sur-Orne. Tel: 31.80.44.05.

POTTERY
Les Ruelles, Clinchamps-sur-Orne. Tel: 31.79.52.33.

Le Château, Laize-la-Ville, nr Clinchamps-sur-Orne. Must book. Tel: 31.79.82.16.

Thury-Harcourt

Ideally situated on the northern tip of Suisse Normande and beside the River Orne, the town has become a popular centre for tourists. Particularly pleasant is the park around the ruined castle, which offers quiet riverside walks. Just to the west, you get some fine views of the Orne at Boucle du Hom, and of the valley and distant heights of Suisse Normande at the chapel at Saint-Joseph, as well as at Mont Pinçon further to the west.

CHEESE
P & A Hamelin, La Motte du Berger, Curcy-sur-Orne, nr Thury-Harcourt. Tel: 31.79.77.97.

CIDER ETC.
Paul & Annie Chanu, Saint-Martin-de-Sallen, nr Thury-Harcourt. Tel: 31.79.70.64.

SNAILS
Ferme des Michaelke, Donnay, nr Thury-Harcourt. Tel: 31.78.28.47.

ENAMEL
Jean Opderbeck, Impasse des Lavandières, Thury-Harcourt. Tel: 31.79.70.15.

The 'capital' of Suisse Normande is the ideal centre for enjoying the delights of the picturesque Orne Valley. Its facilities include walking, climbing, riding, fishing, canoeing and hang-gliding. The area is charmingly depicted in Le Musée du Chemin de Fer Miniature.

WHAT TO SEE ...

Pont du Vey, La Lande Viaduct, La Croix de la Faverie, Le Pain de Sucre, L'Eminence and La Promenade des Crêtes – all fine sights for those who enjoy walking. To the west is the impressive Pontécoulant Château, dating from the 16th century, with its English-style park.

WHAT TO LOOK OUT FOR ...

Cider, calvados, *pommeau* and *poiré*. Also goat's cheese, poultry and honey.

WHERE TO GO FOR ...

CIDER ETC.
Daniel Dupont, La Mérouzière, Condé-sur-Noireau, nr Clécy. Tel: 33.96.12.25.

Melles Leboucher, 2 rue du Manoir, Saint-Denis-de-Méré, nr Clécy. Tel: 31.69.07.08.

Léon Nerou, Montbray, Proussy, nr Clécy. Tel: 31.69.09.07.

André Leboucher, Le Vey, nr Clécy. Tel: 31.69.71.02.

CHEESE
Christine Combe, La Cour Mombret, Le Vey, nr Clécy. Tel: 31.69.73.89.

Daniel François, Saint-Omer, nr Clécy. Tel: 31.69.75.57.

POULTRY
Pierre Eudes, Hameau Sébire, Clécy. Tel: 31.69.70.59.

HONEY
Lionel Letellier, Les Ruches de la Suisse Normande, Le Vey, nr Clécy. Tel: 31.69.46.27.

WHERE TO EAT ...

Le Dumont d'Urville, 15 avenue de la Gare, Condé-sur-Noireau, nr Clécy. Tel: 31.69.68.00.

WHERE TO EAT & STAY ...

Au Site Normand, Rue des Chatelets, Clécy. Tel: 31.69.71.05.

Le Cerf, 18 rue du Chêne, Condé-sur-Noireau, nr Clécy. Tel: 31.69.40.55.

Le Moulin du Vey, Clécy. Tel: 31.69.71.08.

Putanges-Pont-Ecrepin

This small town beside the River Orne is an ideal setting-off point for a memorable visit to Les Gorges de Saint-Aubert. As you wend your way along the picturesque and at times spectacular route to Pont-d'Ouilly, look out for the dam at Rabodanges, Roche d'Oëtre (the most mountainous part of Suisse Normande) and the quaintly named Méandre de Rouvrou where you can see the Orne, just a few metres wide, as it passes through the rocks.

WHAT TO LOOK OUT FOR ...

Chocolates filled with calvados-flavoured cream.

WHERE TO GO FOR ...

CALVADOS ETC.
Roger Longuet, La Gautellerie, Les Routours, nr Putanges-Pont-Ecrepin. Tel: 33.35.04.63.

WHERE TO EAT ...

Bar des Amis, Le Bourg, La Forêt-Auvray, nr Putanges-Pont-Ecrepin. Tel: 33.66.23.30.

Athis-de-l'Orne

WHAT TO LOOK OUT FOR ...

Le Bourdelot, a typically Norman dessert made with pastry and apples, and *Charlotte aux pommes et au calvados*. Show on the third Friday of October. Also dairy produce, cheese, cider, calvados and poiré.

WHERE TO GO FOR ...

CIDER ETC.
Norbert Delozier, Le Bourg, Menil-Hubert-sur-Orne, nr Athis-de-l'Orne. Tel: 31.69.80.73.

DAIRY PRODUCE
M & Mme Harivel, GAEC de la Canne, Montilly-sur-Noireau, nr Athis-de-l'Orne. Tel: 33.96.40.67.

Jean Vardon, Ferme de Treillebois, Athis-de-l'Orne. Also cheese. Tel: 33.66.42.04.

DEER
D de Stoppeleire, Les Bourbes, La Lande-Saint-Siméon, nr Athis-de-l'Orne. Tel: 33.66.40.12.

There has for centuries been a cloth industry based in and around the town, which has a 16th century castle now serving mainly as administrative facilities and as home to an interesting museum (Musée du Bocage Normand). A particular feature here is a typical old Norman kitchen. There is also a section devoted to weaving.

WHAT TO SEE ...

To the west, La Prison Royale and museum in Tinchebray and, to the north-west, Mont de Cerisi with fine views of the surrounding countryside and the Rhododendron Festival on the last Sunday in May.

WHAT TO LOOK OUT FOR ...

Duck, particularly *tourte au canard* and foie gras. Other local treats include *Le Gousset* (beef with stuffing accompanied by fried apples, cream and 'flambé au calvados'), *Le Bec* (pastry dessert with rhubarb and apples cooked in a blackcurrant sugar), *La Chifoine* (a calvados-based liqueur with fruits and herbs) and various confectionery. Show in October. Also calvados, cider and pommeau.

WHERE TO GO FOR ...

DUCK
A Poisson, Charcutier, 77 rue du 6 juin, Flers. Tel: 33.65.23.01.

CALVADOS
Rémy Legay, La Monnerie, Cerisy-Belle-Etoile, nr Flers. Tel: 33.66.51.84.

CIDER
François Gontier, Le Mesnil, La Lande-Patry, nr Flers. Tel: 33.65.27.62.

M Renault, GAEC de la Peschardière, La Peschardière, Tinchebray, nr Flers. Tel: 33.66.63.39.

CHIFOINE
Société Mme Peschet & Fils, 52 rue de la République, Flers. Tel: 33.65.20.58.

FOIE GRAS
Mme Isabelle Saillard, L'Aubinière, Montsecret, nr Flers. Tel: 33.66.51.42.

GOAT'S CHEESE
Alain Chevalier, La Martinière, Banvou, nr Flers. Tel: 33.66.99.30.

POULTRY
Jean-Marie Bois, La Gevraisière, Sainte-Opportune, nr Flers. Also jam. Tel: 33.64.45.62.

DEER
Dominique Deveaux, La Bichetière, Tinchebray, nr Flers. Also other produce. Tel: 33.66.61.15.

WHERE TO EAT ...

L'Auberge du Relais Fleuri, 115 rue Schnetz, Flers. Tel: 33.65.23.89.

L'Auberge des Vieilles Pierres, Route de Paris, D924, Flers. Tel: 33.65.06.96.

La Chaumine, Landisacq, nr Flers. Tel: 33.66.12.28.

La Ferté-Macé

This small town is best known for its tripe. If you are visiting, try to catch the colourful market held on Thursdays. The otherwise modern church is notable for its tower, which has survived since the 11th century.

WHAT TO SEE ...

Apart from the church and the municipal museum, you should take a trip to Bagnoles-de-l'Orne, which boasts the largest spa in western France, and its lake and park. The Orne Fire Brigade Museum is also worth seeing. The Château de Couterne is just to the south. For walkers, the Roc au Chien at Tessé-la-Madeleine is a must, with a little train to help the less energetic on their way. To the east lies the village of Carrouges, in the Normandy-Maine Regional Nature Park. Apart from the local craft centre, you should visit the large and impressive château.

WHAT TO LOOK OUT FOR ...

Tripes en brochettes mode Fertoise (cooked in an earthenware vessel called a *pote*) and smoked andouilles. Show in March. Also calvados, cider, pommeau and poiré.

WHERE TO GO FOR ...

TRIPE
Gérard Chatel, 31 Rue Saint-Denis, La Ferté-Macé. Tel: 33.37.11.85.

CALVADOS ETC.
Yves Sallard, Ferme du Champ de la Vallée, nr La Ferté-Macé. Tel: 33.37.45.92.

WHERE TO EAT ...

L'Auberge de la Source, La Péleras, La Ferté-Macé. Tel: 33.37.28.23.

WHERE TO EAT AND STAY ...

La Lorraine Hôtel, Tessé-la-Madeleine, nr La Ferté-Macé. Tel: 33.37.82.04.

Hôtel Saint-Pierre, Rânes, nr La Ferté-Macé. Tel: 33.39.75.14.

Le Manoir du Lys, Route de Juvigny, Bagnoles-de-l'Orne, nr La Ferté-Macé. Tel: 33.37.80.69.

Hôtel Normandie, Avenue de la Ferté-Macé, Bagnoles-de-l'Orne, nr La Ferté-Macé. Tel: 33.30.80.16.

Hôtel Lutétia-Reine Astrid, Boulevard Paul-Chalvet, Bagnoles-de-l'Orne, nr La Ferté-Macé. Tel: 33.37.94.77.

Ceaucé

WHAT TO LOOK OUT FOR ...

Quail, available fresh, in jars and as pâté (also eggs). Also tripe, cider, calvados and pommeau.

WHERE TO GO FOR ...

QUAIL
Dominique & François Williams, La Bichenière, Ceaucé. Tel: 33.38.36.63.

TRIPE
D Leverrier, Boucherie-Charcuterie, Place du Marché, Ceaucé. Tel: 33.38.32.03.

CALVADOS
Philippe Mauger, Le Bordage, Ceaucé. Tel: 33.38.32.29.

CIDER ETC.
GAEC du Clos Normand, Les Artellières, Sept Forges, nr Ceaucé. Tel: 33.38.30.95.

Cider, calvados, pommeau and poiré. Also dairy produce and jam.

CIDER ETC.
Denis Leroy, Ferme de la Noë Rousse, Passais-la-Conception. Also jam. Tel: 33.38.84.11.

Jean-Claude Fourmond, Le Douët-Gasnier, Mantilly, nr Passais-la-Conception. Tel: 33.38.71.63.

Distillerie du Domaine de la Vectière, Mantilly, nr Passais-la-Conception. Tel: 33.38.70.43.

Roger Lemorton, Pont Barrabe, Mantilly, nr Passais-la-Conception. Tel: 33.38.76.60.

F & C Pacory, GAEC des Grimaux, Mantilly, nr Passais-la-Conception. Tel: 33.30.12.06.

Albert Demeslay, Rue de Montgermont, Saint-Fraimbault, nr Passais-la-Conception. Tel: 33.38.89.46.

Alain Dutertre, La Boiserie, Saint-Fraimbault, nr Passais-la-Conception. Tel: 33.38.36.01.

DAIRY PRODUCE
M & D Leroyer, La Poulardière, Saint Fraimbault, nr Passais-la-Conception. Also cider, apple juice & poiré. Tel:33.38.31.96.

HONEY
Perret-Sourkoff, La Source, Fosse Lahaie, Saint Fraimbault, nr Passais-la-Conception. Also royal jelly & cider. Tel: 33.30.83.72.

Built on a rocky sandstone ridge beside the River Varenne, the town offers some fine views of the countryside – known as the Passais – rich with pear orchards. A point of historical interest here is that Domfront was on several occasions 'English', until the French repossessed it for good in 1450. The old walled town, with 13 of the original 24 towers still evident, is well worth a stroll round, with a blend of stone and timber-framed architecture, particularly Rue du Docteur-Barnabé. You can still see the original paving in the pedestrianised Grande-Rue.

Hôtel de Ville, Eglise Notre-Dame-sur-l'Eau and the Jardin Public du Donjon. Travelling west, a curious twin-towered entrance is all that remains of the 16th century manor at La Saucerie.

Galettes (cake), smoked ham, tripe, poiré, calvados, cider and pommeau. Show on the last Saturday of May for poiré, cider etc.

TRIPE
D Leverrier, Boucherie-Charcuterie, 22 rue du Maréchal Foch, Domfront. Tel: 33.38.65.97.

CALVADOS ETC.
Les Chais du Verger Normand, Domfront Gare, Rue du Mont-Saint-Michel, Domfront. Tel: 33.38.53.96.

Calvados Chatel, Place de l'Eglise, La Chapelle-d'Andaine, nr Domfront. Tel: 33.38.23.03.

CIDER & POIRÉ
Rémy Liot, La Pesnière, La Haute-Chapelle, nr Domfront. Tel: 33.30.85.23.

FOIE GRAS
Louis Retoux, La Haudupierre, La Chapelle-d'Andaine, nr Domfront. Also confit & rillette. Tel: 33.38.13.18.

POULTRY
Alfred Monsallier, La Chevairie, Juvigny-sous-Andaine, nr Domfront. Also restaurant. Tel: 33.38.27.74.

WHERE TO EAT ...

L'Egil, Champsecret, nr Domfront. Tel: 33.30.42.87.

La Chevairie, Juvigny-sous-Andaine, nr Domfront. Must book. Tel: 33.38.20.86.

La Nocherie, Saint-Bomer-les-Forges, nr Domfront. Must book. Tel: 33.37.60.36.

WHERE TO EAT & STAY ...

Hôtel de France, Rue du Mont-Saint-Michel, Domfront. Tel: 33.38.51.44.

Lonlay-l'Abbaye

Set in delightful countryside, especially attractive in the spring, this village is home to a well-known biscuit factory, which makes a type of shortbread according to an old recipe. The church was originally part of an 11th century abbey.

WHAT TO LOOK OUT FOR ...
Shortbread.

WHERE TO GO FOR ...
BISCUITS
Biscuiterie de l'Abbaye, Route du Val, Lonlay-l'Abbaye. Tel: 33.38.68.32.

Vire

The history of this town can be traced back to at least the 8th century, when it began to develop around its castle beside the river of the same name. Sadly, little remains of the fortifications. From the ruins of the keep, added in the 12th century, you will get a fine view of the countryside around. Another survivor is the old main gate in the town square, now the clock tower, from which the panorama is even more impressive. Today Vire's main claim to fame is its andouille, a type of chitterling sausage, made by hand using a recipe that dates back a couple of hundred years.

WHAT TO SEE ...

Eglise Notre-Dame (of 13th century origin), the museum dedicated to locals arts, crafts and traditions (including a series of workshops) and Vaux de Vire just to the south-west, an enclosed site on which the former cloth industry flourished. To the west, there is an animal park at Saint-Sever-Calvados, where the adjoining forest includes an old hermits' monastery and a curious dolmen known as La Pierre Coupée (split rock).

WHAT TO LOOK OUT FOR ...

Andouille de Vire. Also tripe, rillettes, ham, trout, camembert, cider, calvados and pommeau. Special market for foie gras from early November to mid-December.

ANDOUILLE
Lucien Asselot, Coulonces, nr Vire.
Tel: 31.68.21.69.

Charles Amand, 5 rue André Halbout,
Vire. Tel: 31.67.01.79.

Pascal Leveille, Charcuterie, Route de
Granville, Saint-Martin-de-Tallevende,
nr Vire. Also ham & trout.
Tel: 31.68.29.55.

TRIPE & RILLETTES
Michel Ruault, Vire. Tel: 31.68.05.78.

CHEESE
Fromagerie de Vire, Route d'Aulnay,
Vire.

FOIE GRAS
Jacques Lefeuvre, La Blanquière,
La Graverie, nr Vire. Tel: 31.68.40.47.

Nicole Pellerin, La Guézardière,
Saint-Aubin-des-Bois, nr Vire.
Tel: 31.66.05.41.

CIDER ETC.
Claude Foucher, Saint-Martin-de-
Tallevende, nr Vire. Tel: 31.67.14.66.

CALVADOS
Chanu Alcide, Montfroux, Rully,
nr Vire. Tel: 31.68.54.33.

TANNER
Alain Amiard, ZI de la Croix-Verte,
Vassy, nr Vire. Tel: 31.68.59.28.

WHERE TO EAT ...

L'Oasis, Vire. Tel: 31.67.77.77.

Le Manoir de la Pommeraie, Route
de Flers, L'Auverre, Roullours, nr Vire.
Tel: 31.68.07.71.

La Butte aux Cerfs, Lac de la Dathée,
Saint-Germain-de-Tallevende-la-Lande-
Vaumont, nr Vire. Tel: 31.68.30.80.

L'Auberge Saint-Germain, Saint-
Germain-de-Tallevende-la-Lande-
Vaumont, nr Vire. Tel: 31.68.24.13.

La Petite Fosse, Saint-Germain-de-
Tallevende-la-Lande-Vaumont, nr Vire.
Must book. Tel: 31.67.22.44.

La Saffrie, Montchamp, nr Vire.
Tel: 31.68.41.16.

WHERE TO EAT & STAY ...

Hôtel de France, Rue d'Aignaux, Vire.
Tel: 31.68.00.35.

Hôtel Saint-Pierre, Rue Général
Leclerc, Vire. Tel: 31.68.05.82.

Beny-Bocage

WHAT TO LOOK OUT FOR ...

Goose foie gras and rillettes. Show
in November. Also cheese, dairy
produce, cider, calvados and
pommeau.

WHERE TO GO FOR ...

Foie gras & rillettes
Betrand Père et Fils, La Graverie, Beny-
Bocage.

CIDER ETC.
Serge & Guy Renouf, La Mazure,
Le Tourneur, nr Beny-Bocage.
Tel: 31.68.41.86.

GOAT'S CHEESE
Jean-Luc Martin, La Saffrie, Montchamp,
nr Beny-Bocage. Tel: 31.68.41.16.

DAIRY PRODUCE
Jean Maloin, Lassy, nr Beny-Bocage.
Tel: 31.69.62.34.

Le Mesnil-Auzouf

WHAT TO LOOK OUT FOR ...
Snails and poultry.

WHERE TO GO FOR ...

SNAILS
La Groudière, Le Mesnil-Auzouf (dir. Le Plessis-Grimoult). Tel: 31.77.80.26.

POULTRY
Jean-Marie Vallée, Escures, Saint-Jean-le-Blanc, nr Le Mesnil-Auzouf. Tel: 31.69.60.48.

Aunay-sur-Odon

The speed at which this little town was rebuilt after the events of 1944 – in less than six years – must be something of a record. There is an enormous church here with an interestingly decorated facade. To the west, at Jurques, lies a wooded zoological park which contains some very exotic species of animals.

WHAT TO LOOK OUT FOR ...
Cheese and foie gras.

WHERE TO GO FOR ...

CHEESE
Fromagerie d'Aunay-sur-Odon, L'Abbaye, Aunay-sur-Odon. Tel: 31.77.62.77.

FOIE GRAS
Mme Jacqueline Lalleman, Le Carrefour des Fosses, Brémoy, nr Aunay-sur-Odon. Tel: 31.77.83.22.

WHERE TO EAT ...

Les Saulques, Saint-Georges-d'Aunay, nr Aunay-sur-Odon. Must book. Tel: 31.77.03.51.

WHERE TO EAT & STAY ...

Hôtel de la Place, Grande-Rue, Aunay-sur-Odon. Tel: 31.77.47.46.

Caumont-l'Eventé

WHAT TO SEE ...
Le Souterroscope des Ardoisières (recently opened) is a kind of museum dedicated to things underground – with caves, galleries, lakes etc. It is an impressive display, with a shop and restaurant.

WHAT TO LOOK OUT FOR ...
Cider and calvados. Also goat's cheese, dairy produce, poultry and honey.

WHERE TO GO FOR ...
CIDER ETC.
Cidrerie Dujardin, Cahagnes, nr Caumont-l'Eventé. Tel: 31.77.58.49.

Gilbert Lair, Pressoir Dajon, Dampierre, nr Caumont-l'Eventé. Tel: 31.68.72.30.

CHEESE
Melles Pelcerf, Hameau de Candon, Saint-Germain-d'Ectot, nr Caumont-l'Eventé. Tel: 31.25.00.31.

DAIRY PRODUCE & POULTRY
J-Marie Sénéchal, Hameau Beaumont, Cahagnes, nr Caumont-l'Eventé. Tel: 31.77.82.13.

PIGEONS
Marcel Rabec, Village Les Pelletiers, Dampierre, nr Caumont-l'Eventé. Tel: 31.68.70.32.

BREAD
Raoul Achard, Ferme de la Rivière, Sept Vents, nr Caumont-l'Eventé. Tel: 31.68.70.44.

HONEY
Miel Charozé, La Vacquerie, nr Caumont-l'Eventé. Tel: 31.77.40.79.

ANGORA WOOL
Brigitte Monroty, Route de Saint-Lô, La Vacquerie, nr Caumont-l'Eventé. Tel: 31.77.46.85.

Villers-Bocage

Now served by a bypass, this small town contains some unusual modern structures, including the church and the covered market.

WHAT TO LOOK OUT FOR …
Calvados, cider and pommeau.

WHERE TO GO FOR …
CALVADOS ETC.
Alain Aubrée & Jean-Paul Vuilmet, Le Clos d'Orval, Amayé-sur-Seulles, nr Villers-Bocage. Also museum. Tel: 31.77.02.87.

WHERE TO EAT & STAY …
Les Trois Rois, 2 place Jeanne d'Arc, Villers-Bocage. Tel: 31.77.00.32.

Noyers-Bocage

WHAT TO LOOK OUT FOR …
Terrine de campagne (country pâté). Show in March.

WHERE TO GO FOR …
POTTERY
Atelier Déco, Chemin de l'Eglise, Missy, nr Noyers-Bocage. Tel: 31.77.89.10.

WEAVING
Etienne Pasquet, Hameau d'Ourville, Hottot-les-Bagues, nr Noyers-Bocage. Tel: 31.80.81.69.

WOOD SCULPTURE
Pierre Girardy, Route de Juaye-Mondaye, Lingèvres, nr Noyers-Bocage. Tel: 31.08.19.26.

WHERE TO EAT …
L'Auberge de la Cordière, Bellejambe, Noyers-Bocage. Tel: 31.77.97.38.

WHERE TO EAT & STAY …
Le Relais Normand, N175, Noyers-Bocage. Tel: 31.77.97.37.

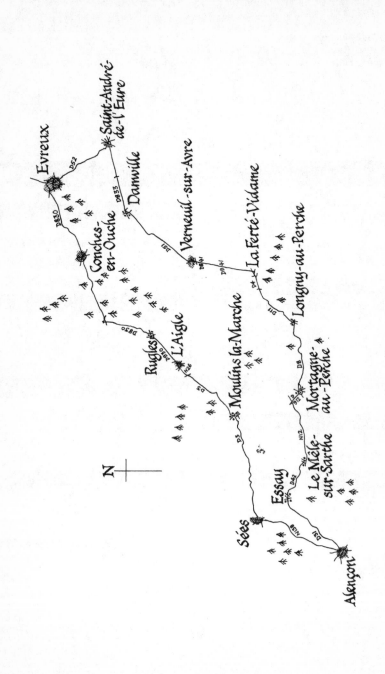

Norman Perche

This tour, which starts from Evreux, takes in much of the picturesque forest and woodland scenery that dominates the southern part of Eure and the eastern corner of Orne, a small region known as the Norman Perche. Here oak and beech trees abound, as do the 'fortified' manor houses which, in stark contrast to those in the Pays d'Auge, are like little castles. The rich meadows which punctuate the forest landscape provide ideal land for cattle – and the raising of the Pecherons heavy horses. A generous range of specialities includes the *cervelas* of L'Aigle, the *brioche* of Moulins-la-Marche and the *boudin* (*blanc* and *noir*).

YOUR ROUTE ...

D830 from Evreux to Conches-en-Ouche & Rugles.

D930 to L'Aigle.

N26 then D3 to Moulin-la-Marche & Sées.

N138 to Alençon.

D31 to Essay.

D42 to Le Mêle-sur-Sarthe.

N12 to Mortagne-au-Perche.

D8 to Longny-au-Perche.

D11 then D4 to La Ferté-Vidame.

D941 then D841 to Verneuil-sur-Avre.

D51 to Damville.

D833 to Saint-André-de-l'Eure.

D52 to Evreux.

Evreux

The administrative capital of Eure on the River Iton, this agricultural market centre has experienced a long history of destruction and rebuilding. The cathedral has undergone different phases of construction dating back to the 12th century but particularly noteworthy are the stained glass and carved wood screens. The former bishop's house next door now contains an interesting museum covering the history and geography of the area. L'Eglise Saint-Taurin contains a wonderful 13th century shrine to the saint.

WHAT TO SEE ...

Cathédrale Notre-Dame, the municipal museum, Eglise Saint-Taurin, Promenade des Remparts and Tour de l'Horloge.

WHERE TO GO FOR ...

CIDER
Etienne Van Tornhout, Le Clos Cerisey, Gauciel, nr Evreux. Tel: 32.67.02.23.

Jacky Desmonts, 5 allée des Chênes, Le Bois-de-l'Etoile, Caugé, nr Evreux. Also honey. Tel: 32.37.18.40.

FOIE GRAS
Maurice Radenac, 10 rue de Planterose, Claville, nr Evreux. Tel: 32.34.05.19.

POULTRY
Guy George, 2 rue de l'Eglise, Vaux-sur-Eure, nr Evreux. Tel: 32.36.61.65.

J-Pierre Metayer, 6 rue Moulin-Sagent, Saint-Aquilin-de-Pacy, nr Evreux. Tel: 32.36.00.89.

Marc Vancaeyzelle, Le Bois Milon, Le Cornier, nr Evreux. Tel: 32.36.81.15.

FRUIT & VEGETABLES
Patrick de Wever, Rue des Hautes-Terres, Sacquenville, nr Evreux. Tel: 32.34.93.78.

Yves Join-Lambert, 2 rue de la Ferme, Angerville-la-Campagne, nr Evreux. Tel: 32.28.96.15.

A Thouvignon, Folleville, Ormes, nr Evreux. Tel: 32.35.45.19.

HONEY
Jacques Bureau, 68 rue Aristide-Briand, Menilles, nr Evreux. Tel: 32.26.11.11.

WHERE TO EAT ...

Le Jardin d'Elodie, 11 rue de la Harpe, Evreux. Tel: 32.38.08.66.

La Gazette, 7 rue Saint-Sauveur, Evreux. Tel: 32.33.43.40.

Le Français, Place Clémenceau, Evreux. Tel: 32.33.53.60.

Le Saint-Nicholas, 38 rue Aristide-Briand, Gravigny, nr Evreux. Tel: 32.38.35.15.

Ferme de l'Eglise-de-Coulonges, Sylvains-les-Moulins, nr Evreux. Must book. Tel: 32.34.52.46.

WHERE TO EAT & STAY ...

Hôtel de France, 29 rue Saint-Thomas, Evreux. Tel: 32.39.09.25.

Hôtel de la Biche, Place Saint-Taurin, Evreux. Tel: 32.38.66.00.

La Ferme de Cocherel, Route de la Vallée-d'Eure, Cocherel, nr Evreux. Tel: 32.36.68.27.

Le Château de Brécourt, Route de Brécourt, Douains, nr Evreux. Tel: 32.52.40.50.

This town lies in an attractive woodland setting on the northern limit of the Forêt de Conches, encircled by the River Rouloir. The features of the church (Saint-Foy) are the tall spire made of wood and lead, numerous gargoyles, some delightful statues and seven remarkable stained-glass windows – dating from the 16th century and stretching across more than 10 metres. The town hall doorway was that of the old castle, ruins of which you can see in the adjoining park.

WHERE TO GO FOR ...

DAIRY PRODUCE
Bruno Dorchies, 1 rue du Stade, La Vielle-Lyre, nr Conches-en-Ouche. Tel: 32.30.91.46.

Didier Duedal, Le Boshion, Orvaux, nr Conches-en-Ouche. Tel: 32.30.13.43.

FOIE GRAS
Brigitte Andrieux, Le Village, Le Chesne, nr Conches-en-Ouche. Tel: 32.29.85.72.

Gaël Garnier, Nuisement, Manthelon, nr Conches-en-Ouche. Tel: 32.30.96.90.

Jean-Bernard Juin, Romilly-la-Puthenaye, nr Conches-en-Ouche. Tel: 32.30.22.28.

B Lamy-Le Goff, Valeuil, nr Conches-en-Ouche. Tel: 32.30.96.26.

POULTRY
Armel Le Cam, Romilly-la-Puthenaye, nr Conches-en-Ouche. Tel: 32.30.03.02.

WHERE TO GO FOR ...

FOIE GRAS
Jean-Marc Dessay, Herponcey, Rugles. Tel: 32.24.64.60.

FRUIT PRODUCE
Georges de Wever, Bois Arnault, nr Rugles. Tel: 32.24.68.49.

WHERE TO EAT ...

Ferme Auberge de la Pommeraie, Juignettes, nr Rugles. Must book. Tel: 33.34.91.84.

La Marigotière, Notre-Dame-du-Hamel, nr Rugles. Tel: 32.44.58.11.

One of the main towns in the Upper Risle Valley and a metal work centre, L'Aigle is believed to have got its name when, in the 17th century, the local lord found an eagle's nest on the site where he wanted to build the present castle. Features of the church (Saint-Martin) include its two contrasting towers, some delightful statues and a magnificently carved altarpiece.

WHAT TO SEE ...

A beautiful 17th century château (now the town hall), Eglise Saint-Martin, Musée Marcel-Angot and the 'June 1944: Battle of Normandy' Museum. Also, to the north-east, an ancient church and

13th century priory at Saint-Sulpice-sur-Risle. To the south-west, at Aube, Nouettes Château and Musée Ségur-Rostopchine.

WHAT TO LOOK OUT FOR ...

Cervelas, a lightly smoked pork-based sausage with Calvados, thyme, bay leaves, onions and spices. Best eaten barbecued, grilled with pieces of smoked bacon, *en croute* with apple purée, boiled and served with sauerkraut, or sliced and eaten cold as a starter. The Aiglon Cervelas is honoured each year during a commercial festival the weekend after Ascension Day. Also foie gras, calvados, cider, *pommeau*, *poiré* and apple juice. Special markets for foie gras in early August and mid-December.

WHERE TO GO FOR ...

CERVELAS
C Linte, Charcutier-Traiteur, 6 rue Romain d'Archy, L'Aigle. Tel: 33.24.18.89.

CALVADOS
Les Caves de Normandie, 64 rue Pasteur, L'Aigle. Tel: 33.24.14.54.

CIDER ETC.
M & Mme Raymond Joui, Les Vergers de Champ-Hubert, Irai, nr L'Aigle. Also rooms. Tel: 33.34.21.58.

WHERE TO EAT ...

Le Relais Saint-Simon, opposite the church, Crulai, nr L'Aigle. Tel: 33.34.25.11.

La Ferardière, La Gonfrière, nr L'Aigle. Must book. Tel: 33.34.81.05.

WHERE TO EAT & STAY ...

Hôtel du Dauphin, 28 place de la Halle, L'Aigle. Tel: 33.84.18.00.

Hôtel du Paradis, La Ferté-Frênel, nr L'Aigle. Tel: 33.34.81.33.

Moulins-la-Marche

WHAT TO LOOK OUT FOR ...

Brioche (a sweet bread-cum-cake). The town is known as 'Cité de la Brioche'. National competition in February, followed by supreme championship in April.

WHERE TO GO FOR ...

DEER
Sylvain Lebrun, L'Etoile-de-Fay, Le Moncel, Fay, nr Moulins-la-Marche. Tel: 33.27.76.34.

WHERE TO EAT ...

La Motte, Courtomer, nr Moulins-la-Marche. Must book. Tel: 33.28.40.03.

The town, through which the River Orne flows, has been an episcopal see since Christianity arrived in the year 400 A.D. and its cathedral provides one of the finest examples of 13th century Norman Gothic architecture. The highlights of its interior include the chancel and the stained-glass windows. Also worth a visit are the old episcopal palace, the former abbey, Notre-Dame-de-la-Place, and the old covered market built as a rotunda. There is also a museum containing works of religious art.

WHAT TO SEE …

To the north-west you will find the graceful and moated Château d'O, which symbolises the imagination of early Renaissance architects.

WHAT TO LOOK OUT FOR …

Foie gras. Also cider and apple juice.

WHERE TO GO FOR …

FOIE GRAS
Philippe Beaudouin, La Piquière, Saint-Hilaire-la-Gérard, nr Sées. Tel: 33.27.07.00.

Jean Geslin, Louvigny, Chailloué, nr Sées. Also restaurant. Must book. Tel: 33.27.86.64.

CIDER ETC.
Lycée Agricole, Avenue du 8 mai 1945, Sées. Tel: 33.27.96.08.

WHERE TO EAT …

L'Ile de Sées, Macé, nr Sées. Tel: 33.27.98.65.

La Ferme d'O, Le Château d'O, Mortrée, nr Sées. Tel: 33.35.35.27.

WHERE TO EAT & STAY …

Hôtel Au Normandy, 20 place du Général de Gaulle, Sées. Tel: 33.27.80.67.

L'Ile de Sées, Macé, nr Sées. Tel: 33.27.98.65.

Alençon

This important market town, which has been extensively restored, contains some fascinating old streets and a pedestrian area with half-timbered houses. It is famous for its lace, once locally a thriving industry. Nearby there is some impressive countryside, including Mont des Avaloirs (417 metres high) to the west and, to the south-west, Les Alpes Mancelles. Although the use of the word 'Alps' may be something of an exaggeration, the high rocky ground offers superb scenery and Saint-Cénéri-le-Gérei, Saint-Léonard-des-Bois and Vallée de Misère are all worth visiting.

WHAT TO SEE …

Eglise Notre-Dame (dating from the 14th century), Musée des Beaux-Arts (Fine Arts), Musée de la Dentelle (Lace), Ancien Château (dating from the 14th century), Halle au Blé (Grain Market), Eglise Saint-Léonard and Chapelle Sainte-Thérèse.

Andouillette, in which pork is minced and not cut, and seasoned with nutmeg, parsley, onions, shallots, vinegar and mustard. Also *boudin blanc*. *Concours National d'Andouillettes* and *International de Boudin Blanc* in October. There is a special festival for foie gras at the end of September. Also calvados and pommeau.

WHERE TO GO FOR ...

ANDOUILLETTE ETC.
Ruel, Charcutier-Traiteur, 21 Grande Rue, Alençon. Tel: 33.26.20.24.

CALVADOS ETC.
Distillerie Préaux, Ravigny, nr Alençon. Tel: 33.27.30.18.

HONEY
Georgette Plenet, Le Bourg, Cuissai, nr Alençon. Tel: 33.26.16.71.

WHERE TO EAT ...

L'Escargot Doré, 183 avenue du Général Leclerc, Alençon.
Tel: 33.28.67.67.

Les Glycines, 32 rue Saint-Blaise, Alençon. Tel: 33.26.41.51.

Essay

WHAT TO LOOK OUT FOR ...

Boudin blanc, a type of sausage made with white pork meat, eggs, flour, milk and herbs. Show on the last Sunday of November claims to be the oldest in Normandy. Also cider.

WHERE TO GO FOR ...

CIDER
Jacques Lambert, Corday, Neauphe-sous-Essai, nr Essay. Tel: 33.27.46.21.

Le Mêle-sur-Sarthe

WHAT TO LOOK OUT FOR ...

Boudin blanc à la mode d'Essay and rillettes. Also dairy produce.

WHERE TO GO FOR ...

BOUDIN & RILLETTES
Chartier, Charcutier-Traiteur, 2 place du Général de Gaulle, Le Mêle-sur-Sarthe. Tel: 33.27.63.07.

DAIRY PRODUCE
GAEC de l'Espoir, La Faucherie, La Mesnière, nr Le Mêle-sur-Sarthe. Tel: 33.25.06.45.

The best view of this elevated town with its clusters of brown-tiled roofs is as you approach from the north. The green valley landscape around gives it an ideal setting. Porte Saint-Denis is virtually all that is left of the original old fortifications. Otherwise the 16th century church has some fine woodwork around its altar and an interesting museum recalls the life of the philosopher Alain, who was born here. But the town is probably best known for its *boudin noir*, a type of sausage.

WHAT TO SEE …

Forêt du Perche and Forêt de la Trappe to the north-east, with the isolated 12th century Abbaye de la Trappe and a magnificent 15th century tapestry in the church at Tourouvre.

WHAT TO LOOK OUT FOR …

Boudin noir (like black pudding but softer and much tastier). Show on the third weekend of March during the *Foire au Boudin* (Boudin Festival), the oldest international charcuterie festival in France. Also foie gras, dairy produce, calvados and pommeau.

WHERE TO GO FOR …

BOUDIN
Lamy-Gaisnon, Charcutier-Traiteur, 12 place de l'Eglise, Bazoches-sur-Hoëne, nr Mortagne-au-Perche. Tel: 33.25.12.79.

C Guillochon, Charcutier, 50 place du Général de Gaulle, Mortagne-au-Perche. Tel: 33.25.16.43.

FOIE GRAS
Roger Hy, Montgazon, Bures, nr Mortagne-au-Perche. Tel: 33.27.25.31.

Daniel Chartrain, La Motte, Corbon, nr Mortagne-au-Perche. Tel: 33.83.84.30.

Gérard Gosselin, Le Perrier, Le Courthenou, La Chapelle-Montligeon, nr Mortagne-au-Perche. Also restaurant. Must book. Tel: 33.83.86.80.

CALVADOS ETC.
Cave de Vieillissement de Mortagne-au-Perche. Tel: 33.73.70.03.

DAIRY PRODUCE
Gilbert Simoen, Ferme de l'Hôtel-Neveu, Courgeon, nr Mortagne-au-Perche. Tel: 33.25.10.67.

POULTRY
Philippe Berard, Caverneau, La Mesnière, nr Mortagne-au-Perche. Tel: 33.25.00.30.

HONEY
J-Jacque Sanseau, Les Mares, Champs, nr Mortagne-au-Perche. Also cider. Tel: 33.25.73.29.

Longny-au-Perche

This small town enjoys a delightful setting by the River Jambée, with La Forêt de Longny to the east. The pretty 16th century Chapelle de Notre-Dame-de-Pitié has some interesting features and provides a good view of Longny. To the west lies La Forêt de Réno-Valdieu, with some magnificent oak and beech trees more than 250 years old and more than 40 metres high.

WHAT TO LOOK OUT FOR …

Tripe and pâté *forestier* (made with woodland mushrooms). Shows on May 1 (tripe) and the first weekend of October (pâté).

Verneuil-sur-Avre

This 'three-in-one' town on the River Avre has a curious history – originally well fortified with walls and a moat, as were the three districts inside, today these are represented by Rue de la Madeleine, Rue Gambetta and Rue Notre-Dame. All three streets contain some charming examples of the traditional half-timbered architecture.

WHAT TO SEE …

Eglise La Madeleine (particularly the tower and some fine works of art inside) and Eglise Notre-Dame (with its impressive collection of 16th century statues).

WHAT TO LOOK OUT FOR …

Foie gras.

WHERE TO GO FOR …

FOIE GRAS
Lionel Rimbert, GAEC de la Moléculture, Le Petit Mesnil, Verneuil-sur-Avre. Tel: 32.32.05.88.

Denis Baudry, Ferme de Parigny, Condé-sur-Iton, nr Verneuil-sur-Avre. Tel: 32.29.71.14.

Bernard Gaudry, Ferme des Petites-Turgères, Bâlines, nr Verneuil-sur-Avre. Tel: 32.32.30.47.

Daniel Masselin, Buray, La Madeleine-de-Nonancourt, nr Verneuil-sur-Avre. Tel: 32.58.32.06.

DAIRY PRODUCE
Matteys Père & Fils, La Harillière, Gournay-le-Guérin, nr Verneuil-sur-Avre. Also poultry. Tel: 32.32.15.53.

WHERE TO EAT …

L'Auberge Chanteclerc, Bourth, nr Verneuil-sur-Avre. Tel: 32.32.61.45.

Auberge des Bons Enfants, Les Mésangères, Bourth, nr Verneuil-sur-Avre. Tel: 32.32.61.72.

WHERE TO EAT & STAY …

L'Hostellerie du Clos, 98 rue de la Ferté-Vidame, Verneuil-sur-Avre. Tel: 32.32.21.81.

Le Moulin de Bâlisne, N12, Bâlines, nr Verneuil-sur-Avre. Tel: 32.32.03.48.

Saint-André-de-l'Eure

WHERE TO GO FOR …

CIDER
François Perdereau, Beaufort, Lignerolles, nr Saint-André-de-l'Eure. Tel: 32.37.34.37.

Milcent Père & Fils, GAEC de Faverolles, Lignerolles, nr Saint-André-de-l'Eure. Also poultry. Tel: 32.37.35.65.

Raymond Cissey, Le Favril, Coudres, nr Saint-André-de-l'Eure. Tel: 32.37.29.31.

GOAT'S CHEESE
Elise Buisson, Rue Mare-du-Four, Le Plessis Hébert, nr Saint-André-de-l'Eure. Tel: 32.26.06.55.

WHERE TO EAT …

Auberge de Maître Corbeau, Place du Marché, Ezy-sur-Eure, nr Saint-André-de-l'Eure. Tel: 37.64.73.29.

Ferme de la Côte-Blanche, Ezy-sur-Eure, nr Saint-André-de-l'Eure. Must book. Tel: 37.64.73.60.

Laine & Fessier, Ferme Saint-Pierre, Grossoeuvre, nr Saint-André-de-l'Eure. Must book. Tel: 32.37.95.31.

Cotentin

This tour, which begins at Cherbourg, takes you round the Cotentin Peninsula, best known for its diverse coastline, its oyster beds, its dairy produce and its vegetables – and much more besides. This is an area of mixed landscape, from the rugged cliffs around Cap de la Hague and Nez de Jobourg in the north-west corner, to the extensive marshland of the Regional National Park to the south. This is the home of Normandy's oysters – and many other shellfish. It is also the land of early vegetables and of rich pastures from which some of France's best dairy produce originates. In between, the Cotentin woodland is the ideal setting for those granite-built castles and manor houses so typical of this part of Normandy.

YOUR ROUTE ...

D901 from Cherbourg to Hameau-de-la-Mer.
D45 to Auderville.
D401 then D901 to Beaumont-Hague.
D318 to Biville.
D37 then D904 to Les Pieux & Barneville-Carteret.
D903 then D650 then D652 to Lessay.
D900 to Périers.
D971 to Saint-Sauveur-Lendelin & Coutances.
(D44 then D72 to Agon-Coutainville
D650 then D20 to Annoville)
D972 to Saint-Lô.
N174 to Carentan.
N13 to Sainte-Mère-Eglise & Valognes.
D902 then D1 to Saint-Vaast-la-Hougue.
D902 to Barfleur.
D901 to Saint-Pierre-Eglise.
D210 then D116 to Cherbourg.

See map overleaf

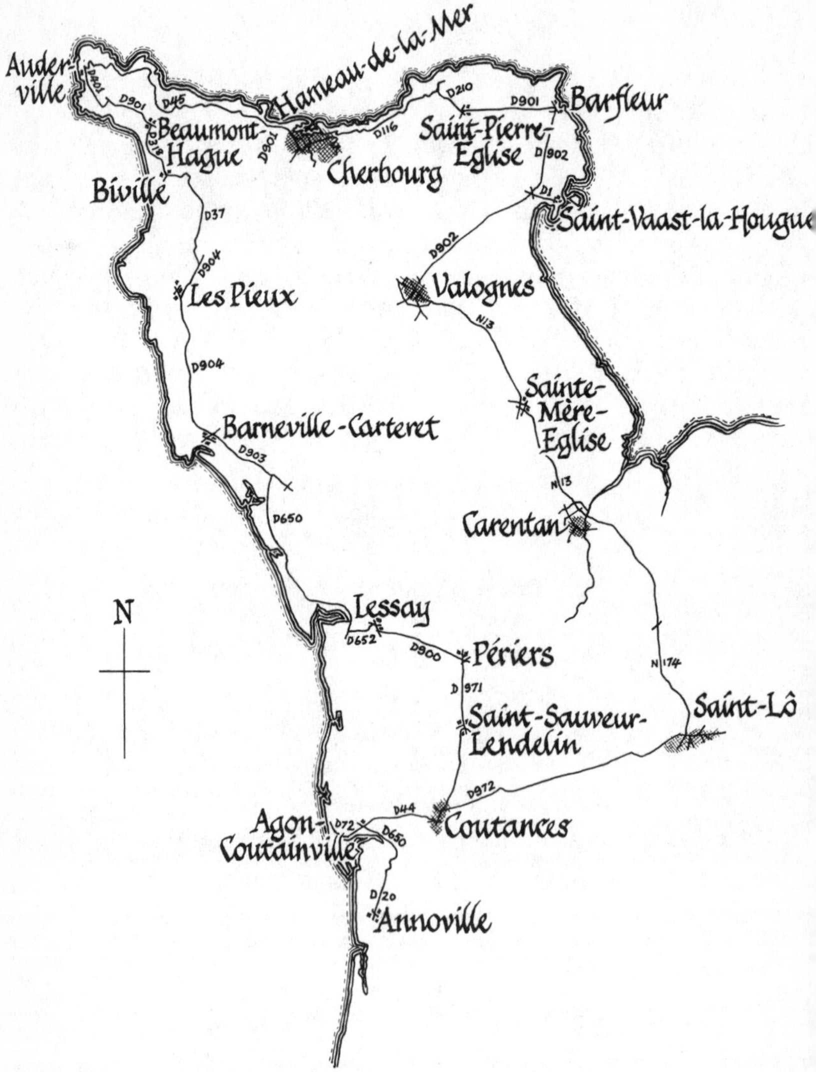
Auderville
Hameau-de-la-Mer
Barfleur
D401
D901
D45
D210
D901
Beaumont-Hague
D318
D901
D116
Saint-Pierre-Eglise
Cherbourg
D902
Biville
D1
Saint-Vaast-la-Hougue
D37
D902
D904
Les Pieux
Valognes
N13
D904
Sainte-Mère-Eglise
Barneville-Carteret
D903
N13
D650
Carentan
N
Lessay
D652
D900
Périers
N174
D971
Saint-Sauveur-Lendelin
Saint-Lô
D972
D44
Agon-Coutainville
D72
Coutances
D650
D20
Annoville

The town is probably best known for its naval base (currently being run down) and as a stepping-off point for transatlantic liners, in addition to welcoming ferries from England and Ireland. It also has a large – and expanding – marina for leisure craft.

WHAT TO SEE ...

Fort du Roule, a key German stronghold during the Second World War, offers fine views of the town and harbour. Le Musée de la Guerre et de la Libération is also worth a visit, as are Le Musée Thomas-Henry (art) and the tropical plants in Le Parc Emmanuel-Liais. To the east of the town, you can enter the lush park of the Renaissance château at Tourlaville, where there is also the Chantereyne Maritime Museum. Just to the south of Bretteville is the curious Allée Couverte, a 4000-year-old burial site. There are several good viewpoints to the west of Cherbourg, particularly at Querqueville and Le Rocher du Castel-Vendon. En route, you can pass by the romantic Nacqueville Château and park, and the curious Dur-Ecu Manoir.

WHERE TO GO FOR ...

CHOCOLATES
B Paillaud, 43 bis rue Maréchal-Foch, Cherbourg. Tel: 33.43.04.76.

BREAD & PASTRIES
Jacques Guesdon, Boulangerie du Parc, 14 rue Emmanuel-Liais, Cherbourg. Tel: 33.53.58.91.

WHERE TO EAT ...

Café de Paris, 40 quai de Caligny, Cherbourg. Tel: 33.43.12.36.

Le Faitout, 25 rue Tour Carré, Cherbourg. Tel: 33.04.25.04.

L'Orée des Bois, 2 place de la République, Cherbourg. Tel: 33.04.72.20.

Le Petit Marché, 59 rue au Blé, Cherbourg. Tel: 33.53.67.64.

Le Grandgousier, 21 rue de l'Abbaye, Cherbourg. Tel: 33.53.19.43.

La Cendrée, 18-20 passage Digard, Cherbourg. Tel: 33.93.67.04.

L'Ancre Dorée, 27 rue de l'Abbaye, Cherbourg. Tel: 33.93.98.38.

L'Arnaque, Vallée de Quincampoix, La Glacerie, Cherbourg. Tel: 33.20.50.62.

La Mare Aubert, Le Pont, Martinvast, nr Cherbourg. Tel: 33.52.11.14.

L'Auberge de l'Atre, Haut de Tabarin, Martinvast, nr Cherbourg. Tel: 33.52.03.12.

Le Landemer, Urville-Nacqueville, nr Cherbourg. Tel: 33.03.43.00.

WHERE TO EAT & STAY ...

Hôtel Mercure (L), Gare Maritime, Cherbourg. Tel: 33.44.01.11.

Quality Hôtel (L), Rue Georges-Sorel, Quartier Maupas, Cherbourg. Tel: 33.43.72.00.

Hôtel Chantereyne (M), Port de Plaissance, Cherbourg. Tel: 33.93.02.20.

La Régence (M), 42 quai de Caligny, Cherbourg. Tel: 33.43.05.16.

Ambassadeur Hôtel (M), 22 quai de Caligny, Cherbourg. Tel: 33.44.10.00.

Hôtel Le Curie (M), 12-14 rue Pierre-Curie, Octeville, nr Cherbourg. Tel: 33.97.31.00.

WHERE TO STAY ...

Hôtel Beauséjour (M), 26 rue Grande Vallée, Cherbourg. Tel: 33.53.10.30.

Hôtel de la Gare (B), 10 place Jean-Jaurès, Cherbourg. Tel: 33.43.06.81.

Auderville

This delightful village, with neighbouring Jobourg, has been left untouched and almost forgottten by the passage of time. The coastal scenery around – notably Le Cap de la Hague, La Baie d'Ecalgrain and Le Nez de Jobourg – is quite spectacular and on a fine day there are magnificent views over to the Channel Islands.

WHERE TO EAT ...

Auberge de Goury, Port de Goury, Auderville. Tel: 33.52.77.01.

Auberge des Grottes, Le Nez de Jobourg, nr Auderville. Tel: 33.52.71.44.

WHERE TO EAT & STAY ...

Hôtel de la Hague, Le Bourg, Auderville. Tel: 33.52.77.67.

Les Pieux

WHAT TO LOOK OUT FOR ...

Calvados, cider, *pommeau* and apple juice. Also dairy produce.

WHERE TO GO FOR ...

CALVADOS ETC.
Théo Capelle, Sotteville, nr Les Pieux. Tel: 33.04.41.17.

Emile Mahieu, Hameau Mesles, Bricquebosq, nr Les Pieux. Tel: 33.04.41.19.

DAIRY PRODUCE
Yves-Marie & Mathilde Connefroy, La Mielle, Le Rozel, nr Les Pieux. Tel: 33.52.41.62.

WHERE TO EAT ...

La Miloreine, La Gare, Couville, nr Les Pieux. Tel: 33.52.02.53.

WHERE TO EAT & STAY ...

Hôtel de la Falaise, Diélette, nr Les Pieux. Tel: 33.04.08.40.

Le Baligan, Diélette, nr Les Pieux. Tel: 33.52.59.55.

This popular resort includes a spectacular rocky headland and a harbour from which you can travel to the Channel Islands. There are several fine viewpoints, including the lighthouse.

WHAT TO SEE ...

The 11th century church with fortified tower and, in nearby Portbail, the sandy beaches, a 13-arch bridge and the Eglise Notre-Dame, built during the 11th century on the site of a 6th century abbey.

WHERE TO GO FOR ...

CIDER ETC.
Michel Jean, 11 rue Saint-Germain, Barneville-Carteret. Tel: 33.45.61.29.

Auguste Lefevre, La Charlerie, Saint-Georges-de-la-Rivière, nr Barneville-Carteret. Tel: 33.53.82.82.

POULTRY
Cécile Hamel, Le Grand Breuil, Les Moitiers d'Allonne, nr Barneville-Carteret. Tel: 33.04.91.46.

VEGETABLES
R & G Leconte-Laurent, La Hurette, Beaubigny, nr Barneville-Carteret. Tel: 33.04.33.15.

WHERE TO EAT & STAY ...

Hôtel de la Marine, 11 rue de Paris, Barneville-Carteret. Tel: 33.53.83.31.

Le Carteret, 5 avenue de la République, Carteret, Barneville-Carteret. Tel: 33.04.95.63.

This small town is best known for its superbly restored Romanesque abbey church. To the south lie the famous market gardens of Créances. The extensive patchwork of small fields produces some of the finest carrots and leeks in the whole of France. Also to the south is Château Pirou, originally a wooden fortress but rebuilt in stone in the 12th century and surrounded by a moat. Of particular interest are the Bayeux-style tapestry, the original of which can be viewed only in July and August, and the curious legend of the geese of Pirou. To the north, Mont Castre offers a splendid panorama of the Cotentin Peninsula, a view most rewarding for those willing to tackle the rocky ascent up to the old Roman watch-post.

WHAT TO LOOK OUT FOR ...

Vegetables, smoked ham, camembert cheese, butter and crème fraîche. Also oysters at Bretteville-sur-Ay.

WHERE TO GO FOR ...

CHEESE ETC.
Ets Reaux, Laiterie Fromagerie du Val d'Ay, Lessay. Tel: 33.46.41.33.

OYSTERS
Jacques Frisch, La Pointe du Banc, Bretteville-sur-Ay, nr Lessay. Tel: 33.47.24.65.

Périers

WHAT TO LOOK OUT FOR ...

Cider and dairy produce.

WHERE TO GO FOR ...

CIDER

Yves Lerendu, Cavilly, La Feuillie, nr Périers. Tel: 33.46.62.32.

Georgette & Claude Levaufre, La Tauterie, Vaudrimesnil, nr Périers. Tel: 33.46.60.29.

DAIRY PRODUCE

Cécile & Michel Lenesley, Village Champeaux, Marchésieux, nr Périers. Tel: 33.46.62.54.

André Leroy, La Harivière, Millières, nr Périers. Tel: 33.46.59.76.

WHERE TO EAT & STAY ...

Hôtel de la Poste, 5 rue de la Gare, Périers. Tel: 33.46.64.01.

Saint-Sauveur-Lendelin

WHAT TO LOOK OUT FOR ...

Cider and foie gras.

WHERE TO GO FOR ...

CIDER

Philippe Bourguet, Le Champ Benoit, Le Mesnilbus, nr Saint-Sauveur-Lendelin. Tel: 33.07.67.61.

FOIE GRAS

SCA Elevage de la Taute, La Rihouerie de Bas, Saint-Sauveur-Lendelin. Tel: 33.46.28.75.

WHERE TO EAT ...

Auberge des Bonnes Gens, Le Mesnilbus, nr Saint-Sauveur-Lendelin. Tel: 33.07.66.85.

This hill-top town is dominated by its imperious Gothic cathedral, whose spires soar high above the undulating landscape. Built on the ruins of an 11th century church, its nave and lantern tower are particularly impressive. Look out for the local cheese, bearing the town's name, which is fast gaining the reputation of its more illustrious partners. *Les Cotentines* are special chocolates made here and around the area. In season, Le Jardin des Plantes offers a magnificently colourful floral spread.

WHAT TO SEE ...

The cathedral, Eglise Saint-Pierre, Le Musée Quesnel-Morinière (local collections) and Le Jardin des Plantes. To the north-east is the medieval Gratot Château, painstakingly restored by volunteers. A curious legend surrounds Le Tour de la Fée (fairy).

WHAT TO LOOK OUT FOR ...

Coutances cheese and cider. Also chocolates made by the Meiss family since 1895.

WHERE TO GO FOR ...

CHOCOLATES
B Meiss, 7 rue Saint-Nicholas, Coutances. Tel: 33.46.35.32.

Chevaliers d'Argouges, Le Pavement Gratot, Coutances. Tel: 33.45.89.50.

CHEESE
Fromagerie de Coutances, 93 rue Pont de Soulles, Coutances. Tel: 33.07.19.19.

DAIRY PRODUCE
G & N Langeard, La Barbinière, Ouville, nr Coutances. Tel: 33.46.89.69.

DAIRY PRODUCE & POULTRY
SCEA Delafosse, La Hermanière, Carantilly, nr Coutances.
Tel: 33.56.64.22.

CIDER
Dominique Eve, Lycée Agricole, Coutances. Tel: 33.45.41.10.

Sylvain & Robert Clement, Le Village Vigot, Le Lorey, nr Coutances.
Tel: 33.47.09.60.

Emile Jean, La Campagne, Le Lorey, nr Coutances. Tel: 33.07.63.95.

Philippe Leverrier, Le Manoir de Soulles, Quettreville-sur-Sienne, nr Coutances. Tel: 33.47.61.08.

FRUIT & VEGETABLES
Paul-Emile Begin, La Chevalerie, Camprond, nr Coutances.
Tel: 33.47.80.83.

WHERE TO EAT ...

Restaurant Notre-Dame, 4 rue d'Harcourt, Coutances. Tel: 33.45.00.67.

Restaurant des Tisserands, Cametours, nr Coutances.
Tel: 33.46.10.10.

Le Jules Gommès, Regnéville-sur-Mer, nr Coutances. Tel: 33.45.32.04.

WHERE TO EAT & STAY ...

Hôtel Cositel, Route de Countainville, Coutances. Tel: 33.07.51.64.

Le Parvis, Place du Parvis, Coutances. Tel: 33.45.13.55.

Hostellerie de la Baie, Le Port, Regnéville-sur-Mer, nr Coutances.
Tel: 33.07.43.94.

Hôtel du Bon Vieux Temps, Montmartin-sur-Mer, nr Coutances.
Tel: 33.47.54.44.

Hôtel de la Plage, 1 avenue Aumesle, Hautville-sur-Mer, nr Coutances.
Tel: 33.47.52.33.

Hôtel du Château de la Salle, Montpinchon, nr Coutances.
Tel: 33.46.95.19.

La Voisinière, Savigny, nr Coutances. Tel: 33.07.60.32.

Agon-Coutainville

This popular seaside resort has a long stretch of sandy beach, which at low tide provides an excellent view of oyster beds, for which the area is famous. To the south, the headland stretching to La Pointe-d'Agon is an interesting habitat – of dunes, grasses and conifers. Look out for the curious line of inscribed stones which stand as a memorial to the 18th century writer Fernand Lechanteur. Inland, there is a fine and very ornate statue in the village of Tourville-sur-Sienne of the celebrated admiral of the same name.

WHAT TO LOOK OUT FOR ...

Oysters. Exposed to both strong winds and tides, the oysters of the Côte Ouest, which includes Coutainville, Blainville, Gouville and the coastline above, have a clear shell, a spicy taste and an iodised flavour. More than 14,000 tonnes are harvested each year. Here you can see one of the rare sites on French beaches of literally dozens of tractors with trailers navigating their way through acre upon acre of vast oyster beds when the tide is out, and racing back to shore as it returns.

WHERE TO GO FOR ...

SHELLFISH
Georges Quettier, Zone Conchylicole, Agon-Coutainville. Tel: 33.47.01.77.

René K'Dual, Rue de la Mielle, Gouville-sur-Mer, nr Agon-Coutainville. Tel: 33.47.81.77.

Evelyne & Roger K'Dual, 45 rue de la Mer, Gouville-sur-Mer, nr Agon-Coutainville. Tel: 33.47.80.75.

WHERE TO EAT & STAY ...

Emile Hardy, Place du 28 Juillet, Coutainville. Tel: 33.47.04.11.

L'Azac Motel, Blainville-sur-Mer, nr Agon-Coutainville. Tel: 33.46.24.67.

WHERE TO STAY ...

Hôtel Neptune, Promenoir Jersey, Agon-Coutainville. Tel: 33.47.07.66.

Annoville

WHAT TO LOOK OUT FOR ...

Biscuits, cider, calvados and pommeau.

WHERE TO GO FOR ...

BISCUITS
Biscuiterie L'Annovillaise, Annoville Bourg. Tel: 33.47.50.00.

CIDER ETC.
Jacques Ameline, La Closerie, Annoville. Tel: 33.47.54.42.

The administrative centre of the Manche *département*, this town gained the depressing name of 'The Capital of Ruins' after it was almost completely destroyed in the Allied onslaught against the Germans in the summer of 1944. All that remains visible is a section of the old ramparts and towers which stand as a chilling reminder of the price paid for liberation. L'Eglise Notre-Dame also bears witness to the massive bombardment. Two places of interest are Le Musée des Beaux-Arts and Le Haras, an important breeding centre for racehorses. On the south-west side of the town is the Franco-American Memorial Hospital and the grandiose new Préfecture, aptly nicknamed 'Le Petit Versailles' by the locals.

WHAT TO LOOK OUT FOR ...

Foie gras, smoked ham and dairy produce. Festival of foie gras at the beginning of April.

WHERE TO GO FOR ...

FOIE GRAS
SCEA des Gouleries, Les Gouleries, Dangy, nr Saint-Lô. Tel: 33.56.01.71.

SMOKED HAM
Jacques Lerouxel & Daniel Ruault, Les Jambons d'Antan, Le Bourg, La Chapelle-en-Juger, nr Saint-Lô. Tel: 33.57.68.47.

DAIRY PRODUCE
Antoine Demortreux, Ferme de la Noe, Rouxeville, nr Saint-Lô. Tel: 33.55.70.65.

BREAD
Serge Enée, La Barberie, Le Mesnil-Rouxelin, nr Saint-Lô. Tel: 33.57.00.53.

WHERE TO EAT ...

Le Marignan, Place de la Gare, Saint-Lô. Tel: 33.05.15.15.

La Créperie, 11 rue Alsace-Lorraine, Saint-Lô. Tel: 33.05.17.37.

La Gonivière, Rond-point du 6 Juin, Saint-Lô. Tel: 33.05.15.36.

Le Chant des Oiseaux, Moulin l'Abbé, Route d'Isigny, Saint-Lô. Tel: 33.05.64.38.

Le Péché Mignon, 84 rue du Maréchal Juin, Saint-Lô. Tel: 33.72.23.77.

La Petite Auberge, D999, Candol, nr Saint-Lô. Tel: 33.05.34.11.

Restaurant de la Poste, Place Westport, Marigny, nr Saint-Lô. Tel: 33.55.11.08.

Les Glycines, Saint-Pierre-de-Semilly, nr Saint-Lô. Tel: 33.05.02.40.

L'Auberge de l'Abbatiale, Place du Marché, Cerisy-la-Forêt, nr Saint-Lô. Tel: 33.56.89.23.

WHERE TO EAT & STAY ...

Le Tocqueville (M), 5-7 avenue Briovère, Saint-Lô. Tel: 33.05.08.63.

Hôtel Ibis (M), Place de la Gare, 1 avenue Briovère, Saint-Lô. Tel: 33.05.10.84.

Hôtel Ibis (M), ZA La Chevalerie, Saint-Lô. Tel: 33.57.78.38.

Game Fair (M), Rond-point de la Liberté, Saint-Lô. Tel: 33.56.56.56.

La Crémaillère (B), Place de la Préfecture, Saint-Lô. Tel: 33.57.14.68.

Château de la Roque (M), Hébécrevon, nr Saint-Lô. Tel: 33.57.33.20.

Le Château de l'Abbaye (L), 1 rue des Sangles, Cerisy-la-Forêt, nr Saint-Lô. Tel: 33.55.71.73.

Le Château d'Agneaux (L), Avenue Sainte-Marie, Agneaux, nr Saint-Lô. Tel: 33.57.65.88.

Carentan

An important market town and a centre for the dairy industry in the Cotentin Peninsula. The octagonal spire of the Gothic Eglise Notre-Dame dominates the surrounding landscape. Of particular interest are the 14th century arcades of the old market in Place de la République, and L'Hôtel de Ville.

WHAT TO LOOK OUT FOR ...

Calvados, cider and pommeau. Also dairy produce.

WHERE TO GO FOR ...

CALVADOS ETC.
Hérout Fils, Cantepie, Auvers, nr Carentan. Tel: 33.42.04.24.

M Debrix, GAEC du Promenoir, Coigny, nr Carentan. Tel: 33.42.09.02.

DAIRY PRODUCE
Hervé Lefort, Le Pommier, Liesville-sur-Douve, nr Carentan. Tel: 33.71.01.60.

Le Panier Normand, Saint-Hilaire-Petitville, nr Carentan.

CHEESE
Chèvrerie du Mesnil, Saint-Hilaire-Petitville, nr Carentan. Tel: 33.42.32.00.

WHERE TO EAT & STAY ...

L'Aire de la Baie, N13, Les Veys, Carentan. Tel: 33.42.00.99.

Hôtel du Commerce et de la Gare, 34 rue de la Gare, Carentan. Tel: 33.42.02.00.

Hôtel Vipotel, Rue du Mesnil, Saint-Hilaire-Petitville, nr Carentan. Tel: 33.71.11.11.

WHERE TO STAY ...

Hôtel Le Vauban, Place Vauban, Carentan. Tel: 33.71.00.20.

Sainte-Mère-Eglise

Nestling at the heart of traditional cattle-breeding country, this little town made tragic history on the night of the D-Day Landings in June 1944 when American troops fatally parachuted into its midst – and that of the German soldiers. The church provides a touching memorial to this unfortunate episode in the form of a stained-glass window and a dummy parachutist suspended on the belfry. Opposite is the fascinating Musée des Troupes Aéroportées. From here Utah Beach, with its monuments and museum, is just a short drive away. On a more peaceful note, the Cotentin Farm Museum recreates rural life at the beginning of the century.

WHAT TO SEE ...

Musée de la Ferme du Cotentin, which also has rooms, the church, Musée des Troupes Aéroportées and Utah Beach, a short drive away.

WHERE TO EAT ...

Auberge de l'Ouve, Longuerac, Les Moitiers-en-Bauptois, nr Sainte-Mère-Eglise. Tel: 33.21.16.26.

WHERE TO EAT & STAY ...

Hôtel Le Sainte-Mère, N13, Richedoux, Sainte-Mère-Eglise. Tel: 33.21.00.30.

Much rebuilt following the last war, this important market town still contains evidence of its past, including some Roman ruins, churches dating back to the 11th century and some fine 18th century mansions, including Hôtel de Beaumont, Hôtel de Granval-Caligny and Hôtel de Thieuville, which houses two museums – dedicated to brandy and leather. Make sure you pay a visit to Le Musée Régional du Cidre, which provides some fascinating exhibits and is housed in the 15th century Logis du Grand Quartier.

WHAT TO LOOK OUT FOR ...

Cider, Calvados, pommeau and *poiré*. Also special market for foie gras at the end of November.

WHERE TO GO FOR ...

CIDER ETC.
Cooperative de Sottevast, nr Valognes. Tel: 33.41.96.46.

Ets Dupont, Saint-Joseph, nr Valognes. Tel: 33.40.19.27.

Michel Hamel, Les Petits Bois, Saint-Joseph, nr Valognes. Tel: 33.40.17.12.

Louis Frigout, La Croix Jacob, Négreville, nr Valognes. Tel: 33.40.22.37.

Musée Régional du Cidre, Rue du Petit-Versailles, Valognes. Tel: 33.40.22.73.

Musée des Vieux Métiers, Rue Pelouze, Valognes. Tel: 33.40.26.25.

WHERE TO EAT ...

L'Agriculture, 16 rue Léopold-Delisle, Valognes. Tel: 33.95.02.02.

WHERE TO EAT & STAY ...

Le Haut Gallion, Route de Cherbourg, Valognes. Tel: 33.40.40.00.

Hôtel de l'Agriculture, 16-18 rue Léopold-Deslisle, Valognes. Tel: 33.95.02.02.

Grand Hôtel du Louvre, 28 rue des Religieuses, Valognes. Tel: 33.40.00.07.

Le Château de Quinéville, Quinéville, nr Valognes. Tel: 33.21.42.67.

Saint-Vaast-la-Hougue

This pretty fishing port with a fortified harbour boasts some of the finest oysters in the region. Local artist Paul-José Gosselin has an interesting workshop-cum-museum. The same family runs a fascinating grocery-cum-museum – Caves Saint-Vincent – a veritable 'Alladin's Cave' of the regional produce. Just offshore is L'Ile de Tatihou, with its nature reserve and maritime museum. To the north, La Pointe de Saire offers some fine views, while further panoramic spots and picturesque countryside can be found just inland, to the west of Quetthou.

WHAT TO SEE ...

The lighthouse and Chapelle des Marins, Ile de Tatihou and, to the north, La Pernelle for the view.

WHAT TO LOOK OUT FOR ...

Oysters and vegetables. The Bassin de Saint-Vaast is one of the three principal oyster beds in Normandy. These oysters are famous for their 'nutty' flavour and considered less iodised and more meaty than those of the Côte Ouest. More than 10,000 tonnes are harvested each year.

WHERE TO GO FOR ...

OYSTERS
Francis Helie, 31 rue d'Isamberville, Saint-Vaast-la-Hougue. Tel: 33.54.42.70.

Huitrière de Normandie, 13 rue d'Isamberville, Saint-Vaast-la-Hougue. Tel: 33.54.42.75.

GAEC La Tatihou, Ets Lefèvre, Centre Ostréicole Euromer, Saint-Vaast-la-Hougue. Tel: 33.54.43.04.

Bertrand Pichot, Centre Ostréicole Euromer, Saint-Vaast-la-Hougue. Tel: 33.54.51.93.

Hubert Pignot, 108 rue Maréchal-Foch, Saint-Vaast-la-Hougue. Tel: 33.22.16.03.

Jacky Marin, Centre Ostréicole Euromer, Saint-Vaast-la-Hougue. Tel: 33.20.12.05.

Société Lesdos, 23 rue des Chantiers, Saint-Vaast-la-Hougue. Tel: 33.54.42.13.

Raymond Lepoittevin, Centre Ostréicole Euromer, Saint-Vaast-la-Hougue. Tel: 33.54.52.43.

Jacky Adam, Le Moulin du Dick, Quetthou, nr Saint-Vaast-la-Hougue. Tel: 33.54.19.99.

Costard, Chasse du Gros Chêne, Quetthou, nr Saint-Vaast-la-Hougue. Tel: 33.43.20.51.

R Doublet, Village de Grenneville, Crasville, nr Saint-Vaast-la-Hougue. Tel: 33.54.16.33.

VEGETABLES
Alain Cottebrune, Le Houguet, Réville, nr Saint-Vaast-la-Hougue. Tel: 33.54.47.06.

GENERAL PRODUCE
Caves Saint-Vincent, Rue de Verrüe, Saint-Vaast-la-Hougue. Tel: 33.54.40.06.

WHERE TO EAT ...

Fuschias, 19 rue Maréchal-Foch, Saint-Vaast-la-Hougue. Tel: 33.54.42.26.

Ostrea, Quai Vauban, Saint-Vaast-la-Hougue. Tel: 33.54.54.28.

La Flambée, Route de Barfleur, Quettehou, nr Saint-Vaast-la-Hougue. Tel: 33.54.14.89.

La Panoramique, La Pernelle, nr Saint-Vaast-la-Hougue. Tel: 33.54.13.79.

Tatihou Restaurant, Caserne Numéro 7, Ile de Tatihou, nr Saint-Vaast-la-Hougue. Tel: 33.54.07.20.

La Granitière, 74 rue Maréchal-Foch, Saint-Vaast-la-Hougue. Tel: 33.54.58.99.

Hôtel de France et des Fuschias, 18 rue Maréchal-Foch, Saint-Vaast-la-Hougue. Tel: 33.54.42.26.

Le Moine de Saire, Village de l'Eglise, Réville, nr Saint-Vaast-la-Hougue. Tel: 33.54.46.06.

WHERE TO STAY ...

La Demeure du Perron, Quettehou, nr Saint-Vaast-la-Hougue. Tel: 33.54.56.09.

Barfleur

A fishing port of typical Norman charm, with granite houses and lobster pots decorating the quayside. Among the local stories it is said that the boat in which William the Conqueror travelled to invade England was built here. And another English king – Richard the Lionheart – departed from here to take up his crown.

WHAT TO SEE ...

The squat 17th century church, with a stained-glass window dedicated to Sainte-Mary-Magdalene, who as Julie Postel was born in Barfleur in 1756 and founded the Sisters of the Christian Schools of Mercy in Saint-Saveur-le-Vicomte. You can visit her house, La Maison de Julie Postel, in La Bretonne. Also, to the north, Gatteville-le-Phare with its interesting church, and the lighthouse at La Pointe de Barfleur, the tallest in France, which offers a superb panorama. And to the south, the church at Montfarville, dating back to the 13th century.

WHERE TO STAY ...

Hôtel le Conquérant, 16-18 rue Saint-Thomas-Beckett, Barfleur. Tel: 33.54.00.82.

Saint-Pierre-Eglise

This little town has a pleasant church with a 12th century doorway, though the rest is quite a few centuries younger. There is a château as well. From the nearby coast you can enjoy some excellent views – at Raz du Cap-Lévy, Pointe du Brulay and Anse du Brick (literally Brick Bay).

WHERE TO GO FOR ...

TROUT
Jean-Marc Duchemin,
Le Vieux Moulin, Fermanville,
nr Saint-Pierre-Eglise. Tel: 33.54.66.92.

WHERE TO EAT ...

Au Bouquet de Cosqueville, Cosqueville, nr Saint-Pierre-Eglise. Tel: 33.54.32.81.

La Maison Rouge, Anse du Brick, Maupertus-sur-Mer, nr Saint-Pierre-Eglise. Tel: 33.54.33.50.

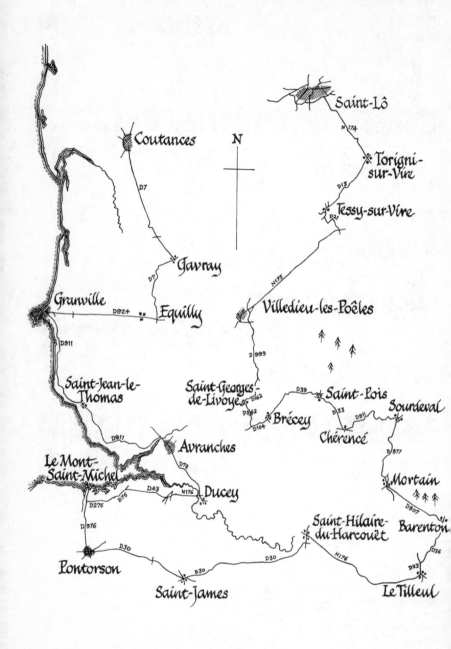

Manche

This tour, which extends south from Cotentin, takes in the rest of the *département* of Manche. Picking up the route from either Coutances or Saint-Lô, you will pass through the charming green and wooded countryside, particularly to the south-east. Your pleasures will include the spectacular sight of Le Mont-Saint-Michel, and the fascinating and at moments rugged landscape around Barenton and Mortain. Do not forget to make a stop at Villedieu-les-Poêles to look at the copper and pewter making. And, of course, everywhere there is cider and calvados and the usual variety of culinary delights waiting to satisfy the finest palate.

YOUR ROUTE ...

D7 from Coutances to Gavray & Equilly.

D924 to Granville.

D911 to Saint-Jean-le-Thomas & Avranches.

D78 to Ducey.

N176, D43, D75 then D275 to Le Mont-Saint-Michel.

D976 to Pontorson.

D30 to Saint-James & Saint-Hilaire-du-Harcouët.

N176 to Le Teilleul.

D32 then D36 to Barenton.

D907 to Mortain.

D977 to Sourdeval.

D911 then D33 to Saint-Pois.

D39 to Brécey, then D104/ D362 to Saint-Georges-de-Livoye.

D162 then D999 to Villedieu-les-Poêles.

N175 then D21 to Tessy-sur-Vire.

D13 to Torigni-sur-Vire.

N174 to Saint-Lô.

Gavray

WHAT TO LOOK OUT FOR ...

Calvados, cider and *pommeau*. Also smoked *andouille*, dairy produce and honey.

WHERE TO GO FOR ...

CALVADOS ETC.
Roland Venisse, GAEC des Deux Vallées, La Butte, La Meurdraquière, nr Gavray. Tel: 33.61.31.52.

CIDER & DAIRY PRODUCE
Delphine Vastel, La Grenterie, La Meurdraquière, nr Gavray. Tel: 33.90.26.45.

DAIRY PRODUCE
Etiennette Legallais, La Pinotière, Le Mesnil Roguès, nr Gavray. Tel: 33.61.38.98.

HONEY
Jean-Pierre Legrand, La Percehaye, La Meurdraquière, nr Gavray. Tel: 33.61.44.25.

ANDOUILLE
B Boscher, Pont-de-la-Baleine, Saint-Denis-le-Gast, nr Gavray. Tel: 33.61.44.20.

WHERE TO EAT ...

Auberge du Mesnil-Roguès, Le Mesnil Roguès, nr Gavray. Tel: 33.61.37.12.

WHERE TO EAT & STAY ...

La Verte Campagne, Le Hameau Chevalier, Trelly, nr Gavray. Tel: 33.47.65.33.

Auberge de l'Abbaye, Hambye, nr Gavray. Tel: 33.61.42.19.

Hôtel Saint-Evremond, Saint-Denis-le-Gast, nr Gavray. Tel: 33.61.44.42.

Granville

Well-known for its carnival, this seaside resort built on and around a mass of rock has been called the Monaco of the North, although it does lack some of the glamour and certainly the weather! Nevertheless it has its followers – and its charm. There is a busy little fishing port, ferries to Les Iles Chausey and the Channel Islands and a marina. The Upper Town (Haute Ville) perched on the headland is particularly impressive with its church (L'Eglise Notre-Dame) and museum (Musée du Vieux Granville). You will get some magnificent views from La Pointe du Roc – on a fine day as far as the coast of Brittany. And if you are looking for a little peace and quiet, the ideal spot is the Christian Dior Garden, once belonging to the couturier's family.

WHAT TO SEE ...

Haute Ville, Eglise Notre-Dame, Musée du Vieux Granville (including pottery and costumes), Musée Richard Anacréon (art), Shell Wonderland, Mineral Palace and Butterfly Garden, Aquarium and Waxwork Museum. To the southeast lie the ruins of the 12th century Abbaye de la Lucerne and a church in a delightful valley setting.

WHAT TO LOOK OUT FOR ...

Stuffed clams, cider, calvados and pommeau.

WHERE TO GO FOR ...

CIDER ETC.
Ferme de l'Hermitière, Saint-Jean-des-Champs, nr Granville. Also a museum. Tel: 33.61.31.51.

Raymond Leroyer, Le Manoir, Anctoville-sur-Boscq, nr Granville. Tel: 33.50.28.96.

Michel Lefranc, La Rocherie, La Lucerne d'Outremer, nr Granville. Tel: 33.61.52.06.

DAIRY PRODUCE
Gérard Aupinel, GAEC de Crecey, Saint-Pair-sur-Mer, nr Granville. Tel: 33.50.26.20.

WHERE TO EAT ...

Normandy Chaumière, 20 rue Paul-Poirier, Granville. Tel: 33.50.01.71.

La Gentilhommière, 152 rue Couraye, Granville. Tel: 33.50.17.99.

Le Phare, 11 rue du Port, Granville. Tel: 33.50.12.94.

L'Auberge de la Blanche Maison, Bricqueville-sur-Mer, nr Granville. Tel: 33.61.65.62.

La Passerelle, Les Salines, Bricqueville-sur-Mer, nr Granville. Tel: 33.61.65.51.

Auberge des 4 Routes, Bréville-sur-Mer, nr Granville. Tel: 33.50.20.10.

Le Casino, Jullouville-sur-Mer, nr Granville. Tel: 33.61.82.82.

WHERE TO EAT & STAY ...

Hôtel des Bains (L), 19 rue Clémenceau, Granville. Tel: 33.50.17.31.

Hôtel de la Mer (M), 74 rue du Port, Granville. Tel: 33.50.01.86.

La Mougine des Moulins-à-Vent (L), Les Moulins-à-Vent, Bréville-sur-Mer, nr Granville. Tel: 33.50.22.41.

Hôtel de la Gare (M), 1 place Commandant-Godart, Bréhal, nr Granville. Tel: 33.61.61.11.

Game Fair (M), Rond-point de la Rocade, Bréhal, nr Granville. Tel: 33.90.04.00.

Le Relais des Isles (M), Coudeville-Plage, nr Granville. Tel: 33.61.66.66.

Hôtel-Pension Simone et Thérèse (B), 520 rue du Fourneau, Saint-Pair-sur-Mer, nr Granville. Tel: 33.50.11.27.

WHERE TO STAY ...

Le Herel (M), Port de Plaisance, Promenade du Docteur-Lavat, Granville. Tel: 33.90.48.08.

Hôtel Terminus (B), 5 place de la Gare, Granville. Tel: 33.50.02.05.

Hôtel Michelet (B), 5 rue J-Michelet, Granville. Tel: 33.51.01.20.

Hôtel Equinoxe (M), 28 avenue de la Libération, Jullouville, nr Granville. Tel: 33.50.60.82.

Hôtel de la Poste (B), 21 rue de la Mairie, Saint-Pair-sur-Mer, nr Granville. Tel: 33.50.06.38.

Saint-Jean-le-Thomas

WHERE TO GO FOR ...
POULTRY
Jean-Louis Lebrun, Le Bisson,
Ronthon, nr Saint-Jean-le-Thomas.
Tel: 33.48.92.33.

WHERE TO EAT ...
Le Relais Saint-Michel, 2 rue du
Général-de-Gaulle, Saint-Jean-le-
Thomas. Tel: 33.60.39.30.

Le Marquis de Tombelaine,
Champeaux, nr Saint-Jean-le-Thomas.
Tel: 33.61.85.94.

WHERE TO EAT & STAY ...
Hôtel des Bains, 8 allée Clémenceau,
Saint-Jean-le-Thomas. Tel: 33.48.84.20.

Avranches

Much history surrounds this interesting town, which offers some commanding views of the surrounding countryside. Its 8th century bishop Saint Aubert founded Le Mont-Saint-Michel, which dominates the seaboard landscape to the west. More recently, it was from here that the Americans under General Patton launched a decisive offensive against the Germans on 31 July 1944.

WHAT TO SEE ...
La Plate-Forme (from where you can best see Le Mont-Saint-Michel) and the nearby museum, Le Jardins des Plantes and the Patton Monument, whose site is officially American territory. Just to the south, near Le Val-Saint-Père, you will find the Musée de la Seconde Guerre Mondiale.

WHAT TO LOOK OUT FOR ...
Salt-meadow lamb reared at Mont-Saint-Michel Bay on grass impregnated with sea salt. Show in March and April to promote local charcuterie, pastries and all products based on apples and pears. Show in October for various regional products. Show in the first quarter of December for *boudin blanc*, with and without truffles.

WHERE TO GO FOR ...

FOIE GRAS
Jean Bazire, La Lande, Saint-Quentin-sur-le-Homme, nr Avranches.
Tel: 33.60.61.62.

Marie-Claude Briant, La Pitelière, Tirepied, nr Avranches. Tel: 33.60.53.89.

Michel Payen, La Mazure, Saint-Senier-sous-Avranches, nr Avranches.
Tel: 33.58.25.93.

Paul Nove, La Gohannière, nr Avranches. Tel: 33.60.52.33.

POULTRY
Jean-Louis Lebrun, Ronthon, nr Avranches. Tel: 33.48.92.33.

DAIRY PRODUCE
Etienne Bechet, Le Val-Saint-Père, nr Avranches. Tel: 33.58.20.28.

CIDER
Bernard Cocman, La Lande Martel, Juilley, nr Avranches. Tel: 33.60.65.48.

WHERE TO EAT ...

Le Grain de Sel, Le Bourg, Dragey-Ronthon, nr Avranches.
Tel: 33.48.28.48.

WHERE TO EAT & STAY ...

Les Abrincates (M), 37 boulevard du Luxembourg, Avranches.
Tel: 33.58.66.64.

Hôtel du Jardin des Plantes (M), 10 place Carnot, Avranches.
Tel: 33.58.03.68.

Le Gué du Holme (L), Le Bourg, Saint-Quentin-sur-le-Homme, nr Avranches. Tel: 33.60.63.76.

Le Relais du Mont (M), D43, La Buvette, Ceaux, nr Avranches.
Tel: 33.70.92.55.

Le Pommeray (M), Route de la Baie, Ceaux, nr Avranches. Tel: 33.70.92.45.

Auberge de la Selune (M), 2 rue Saint-Germain, Ducey, nr Avranches.
Tel: 33.48.53.62.

Hôtel-Motel des 13 Assiettes (M), Le Val-Saint-Pierre, Pontaubault, nr Avranches. Tel: 33.58.14.03.

WHERE TO STAY ...

Le Moulin de Ducey (L), 1 Grande-Rue, Ducey, nr Avranches.
Tel: 33.60.25.25.

Le Mont-Saint-Michel

The history of this extraordinary monument, built on a small granite island, goes back to the 8th century when the Bishop of Avranches founded an oratory on what was then known as Mont Tombe. The abbey itself, whose spire reaches some 150 metres above sea level, dates from the 11th century. This veritable fortress, which is naturally secured by the dreaded fast and high tides that engulf it, became a place of pilgrimage for all – lay as well as religious, rich as well as poor. Today, the site benefits from its role as one of France's best-known tourist attractions – with hotels, restaurants and souvenir shops lining the steep, narrow route to the abbey. In the village round the lower part of the mount, there are a couple of interesting museums, as well as the Archéoscope – a journey back in time to the mount's origins.

WHAT TO LOOK OUT FOR ...

Omelettes (from the original recipe of Annette Poulard) and salt-meadow lamb.

WHERE TO EAT ...

Auberge du Terroir, Servon, nr Le Mont-Saint-Michel. Tel: 33.60.27.97.

WHERE TO EAT & STAY ...

Le Saint-Pierre (L), Grande-Rue, Le Mont-Saint-Michel. Tel: 33.60.14.03.

Hôtel de la Mère Poulard (L), Grande-Rue, Le Mont-Saint-Michel. Tel: 33.60.14.01.

Hôtel Les Terrasses Poulard (L), Intra Muros, Le Mont-Saint-Michel. Tel: 33.60.14.09.

Hôtel La Croix Blanche (L), Le Mont-Saint-Michel. Tel: 33.60.14.04.

Hôtel Duguesclin (M), Intra Muros, Le Mont-Saint-Michel. Tel: 33.60.14.10.

Altea K Motel (M), Le Mont-Saint-Michel. Tel: 33.60.14.18.

Hôtel de la Digue (M), Le Mont-Saint-Michel. Tel: 33.60.14.02.

Le Relais du Roy (M), Le Mont-Saint-Michel. Tel: 33.60.14.25.

Hôtel Motel Vert (M), Le Mont-Saint-Michel. Tel: 33.60.09.33.

Le Saint-Aubert (M), Le Mont-Saint-Michel. Tel: 33.60.08.74.

Le Manoir de la Roche Torin (L), Courtils, nr Le Mont-Saint-Michel. Tel: 33.70.96.55.

WHERE TO STAY ...

Hôtel du Gué de Beauvoir (B), Beauvoir, nr Le Mont-Saint-Michel. Tel: 33.60.09.23.

This small town, the last before you enter Brittany, has an interesting church said to have been founded by William the Conqueror. Inside, La Chapelle-de-Saint-Sauveur is particularly worth a visit. To the east, Saint-James reveals its history in some old streets and ramparts. Again it was William who created the first settlement here. On the outskirts is the American Cemetry and Memorial.

WHERE TO GO FOR ...

DAIRY PRODUCE
Annick Gedouin, Le Petit Manoir, Servon, nr Pontorson. Tel: 33.60.03.44.

WHERE TO EAT ...

Le Grillon, Pontorson.
Tel: 33.60.17.80.

La Pommeraie, Macey, nr Pontorson.
Tel: 33.60.19.37.

La Petite Bouffe, Saint-James, nr Pontorson. Tel: 33.60.55.38.

WHERE TO EAT & STAY ...

Le Montgomery, 13 rue Couesnon, Pontorson. Tel: 33.60.00.09.

Hôtel La Cave, 37 rue de la Libération, Pontorson. Tel: 33.60.11.35.

Hôtel de Bretagne, 59 rue Couesnon, Pontorson. Tel: 33.60.10.55.

Le Relais Clémenceau, 40 boulevard Clémenceau, Pontorson.
Tel: 33.60.10.96.

Le Sillon de Bretagne, N175, Brée-en-Tanis, nr Pontorson. Tel: 33.60.13.04.

Normandie Hôtel, Place Bagot, Saint-James, nr Pontorson. Tel: 33.48.31.45.

Auberge du Terroir, Le Bourg, Servon, nr Pontorson. Tel: 33.60.17.92.

Saint-Hilaire-du-Harcouët

The most prominent feature of this busy market town is its twin-spired church. To the west, the River Sélune is broken by a series of dams, the most attractive of which is that of Vézins. To the east is the wildlife park at Saint-Symphorien-des-Monts, in the grounds of a former château.

WHAT TO LOOK OUT FOR ...

Saucisse à l'oignon (an onion sausage). Show in June. Also dairy produce, foie gras, cider, Calvados, pommeau and apple juice.

WHERE TO GO FOR ...

SAUSAGE
Michel Huet, Charcutier, 20 avenue du Maréchal Leclerc, Saint-Hilaire-du-Harcouët. Tel: 33.49.11.39.

DAIRY PRODUCE & PORK
Joëlle Martinel, La Cocherie, Lapenty, nr Saint-Hilaire-du-Harcouët.
Tel: 33.49.02.88.

BUTTER
Société Beurrière Besnier Isigny, Le Grand Chemin, Isigny-le-Buat, nr Saint-Hilaire-du-Harcouët.
Tel: 33.48.01.99.

FOIE GRAS
Jean-Marc Belloir, La Houssaye,
Saint-Aubin-de-Terregatte, nr Saint-
Hilaire-du-Harcouët. Tel: 33.48.17.55.

Maurice Angot, La Gasneraie,
Les Biards, nr Saint-Hilaire-du-
Harcouët. Tel: 33.48.01.87.

CIDER ETC.
Fermicalva, Le Grand Chemin, Isigny-
le-Buat, nr Saint-Hilaire-du-Harcouët.
Tel: 33.48.00.16.

GAEC du Pressoir, Les Gondinières,
Montigny, nr Saint-Hilaire-du-Harcouët.
Tel: 33.48.00.98.

Jean-Louis Orvain, Montigny,
nr Saint-Hilaire-du-Harcouët.
Tel: 33.48.03.64.

FRUIT & JAM
André Guepratte, ZA Virey, Virey,
nr Saint-Hilaire-du-Harcouët.
Tel: 33.49.21.95.

Le Sélune, Vézins, nr Saint-Hilaire-du-
Harcouët. Tel: 33.60.50.50.

Le Pic Epeiche, Les Biards, nr Saint-
Hilaire-du-Harcouët. Tel: 33.48.02.45.

Auberge de Mirande, Saint-Aubin-de-
Terregatte, nr Saint-Hilaire-du-Harcouët. Must book. Tel: 33.60.05.46.

Le Cygne, 67 rue Waldeck-Rousseau,
Saint-Hilaire-du-Harcouët.
Tel: 33.49.11.84.

Hôtel La Résidence, 99 rue Waldeck-
Rousseau, Saint-Hilaire-du-Harcouët.
Tel: 33.49.10.14.

Le Relais de la Poste, 11-13 rue de
Mortain, Saint-Hilaire-du-Harcouët.
Tel: 33.49.10.31.

Le Teilleul

Cider, dairy produce, poultry and
foie gras.

CIDER
Vert de Vie, ZA Hôtel Morton,
Le Teilleul. Tel: 33.69.54.58.

DAIRY PRODUCE & POULTRY
M-A Rousseau, La Gortière, Le Teilleul.
Tel: 33.59.43.29.

FOIE GRAS
Annick Davoust, Les Grippes,
Le Teilleul. Tel: 33.59.34.30.

Gilbert Poupion, Saint-Cyr-du-
Bailleul, nr Le Teilleul. Tel: 33.59.43.07.

La Clé des Champs, Route de
Domfront, Le Teilleul. Tel: 33.59.42.27.

Of key interest is La Maison de la Pomme et de la Poire, where you will discover the history and techniques of the production of cider, *poiré* and calvados. Outside there are a couple of orchards and you have the chance to take some refreshment after your visit. A small detour to La Fosse Arthour, just to the north-east, will be well rewarded. Here the River Sconce flows rapidly between steep sandstone banks, forming cascades in places. And there are plenty of good views for those who like scrambling over rocky terrain.

WHERE TO GO FOR ...

CIDER ETC.
Maison de la Pomme et de la Poire, La Logeraie, Barenton. Tel: 33.59.56.22.

DAIRY PRODUCE
Huguette Beauge, Le Haut Theil, Saint-Georges-de-Rouelley, nr Barenton. Tel: 33.59.45.28.

WHERE TO EAT ...

La Vieille Auberge, Saint-Georges-de-Rouelley, nr Barenton. Tel: 33.59.44.14.

WHERE TO EAT & STAY ...

Le Relais du Parc, Rue Pierre-Crestey, Barenton. Tel: 33.59.51.38.

Built on the hillside overlooking the River Cance, the town's main attractions are two spectacular waterfalls in charming rocky woodland settings. Although La Grande Cascade is the more accessible, you should also take the time to see La Petite Cascade. The twisting but not too demanding route over waterside boulders will finally bring its reward.

WHAT TO SEE ...

The 12th century Abbaye Blanche, Eglise Saint-Evroult (with its 7th century Anglo-Irish casket) and, to the north, Le Village Enchanté at Bellefontaine – a veritable world of make-believe in miniature.

WHERE TO GO FOR ...

CIDER ETC.
GAEC Suvigny, Chenilly, Saint-Jean-du-Corail, nr Mortain. Tel: 33.59.08.05.

CIDER & FRUIT
M Filatre, Le Logis, Juvigny-le-Tertre, nr Mortain. Tel: 33.59.38.20.

HONEY
Bernard Terrasson, 38 rue des Ecoles, Juvigny-le-Tertre, nr Mortain. Tel: 33.59.21.18.

WHERE TO EAT ...

Auberge Paysanne La Grange, Village Enchanté, Bellefontaine, nr Mortain. Tel: 33.59.01.93.

WHERE TO EAT & STAY ...

Hôtel de la Poste, 1 place des Arcades, Mortain. Tel: 33.59.00.05.

Le Cheval Blanc, 14 avenue de l'Abbaye Blanche, Mortain. Tel: 33.59.00.60.

Le Relais Sainte-Sophie, Bellefontaine, nr Mortain. Tel: 33.59.01.93.

Sourdeval

There is a delightful meandering drive to the east of this little town through the Vallée de la Sée and on to Saint-Michel-de-Montjoie, from where on a clear day you can see as far as Le Mont-Saint-Michel. Have a look at the intriguing granite exhibits in the woodland park museum.

WHERE TO GO FOR ...

DAIRY PRODUCE & POULTRY
Yves Durand, Le Pont d'Egrenne, Le Fresne-Poret, nr Sourdeval. Tel: 33.59.76.74.

Jeanne Desdoits, Le Val, Vengeons, nr Sourdeval. Tel: 33.59.64.16.

POULTRY
Philippe & Bénédicte Lebrun, La Gallerie, Chérencé-le-Roussel, nr Sourdeval. Tel: 33.59.75.15.

FOIE GRAS
Odile Giroult, La Cour, Vengeons, nr Sourdeval. Tel: 33.59.73.22.

CIDER
Jacques Daunay, La Monnerais, Le Mesnil-Tôve, nr Sourdeval. Tel: 33.59.90.05.

WHERE TO EAT ...

Le Temps de Vivre, 12 rue Saint-Martin, Sourdeval. Tel: 33.59.60.41.

WHERE TO EAT & STAY ...

Hôtel du Centre, Sourdeval. Tel: 33.59.60.48.

Saint-Georges-de-Livoye

WHAT TO LOOK OUT FOR ...

Honey, dairy produce and trout.

WHERE TO GO FOR ...

HONEY
Ruchers des Collines de Normandie, La Touche, Saint-Georges-de-Livoye. Tel: 33.48.62.33.

DAIRY PRODUCE
Patrick Lefebvre, Saint-Georges-de-Livoye. Tel: 33.48.62.33.

TROUT
Alain Sourdin, Le Moulin, Saint-Georges-de-Livoye. Tel: 33.60.91.74.

Villedieu-les-Poêles

This town – also known as the 'City of the Knights of Malta', a fact which is commemorated every four years with a grand procession – has a history of copper-making going back to the 12th century. The word *'poêles'*, incidentally, means pots or frying pans. The other important industries here are bell-making and leather tanning. The medieval origins are still evident, with some delightful little streets, alleyways and courtyards – such as Cour-des-Trois-Rois, Cour-aux-Lys and Cour-aux-Moines – and old buildings. Needless to say, there are the inevitable museums showing the local crafts developed over the years. These include copperware and lace, pewter, Norman furniture and clocks. The workshops are worth a visit, as is La Fonderie de Cloches, the Bell Foundry.

WHAT TO SEE ...

To the north, the impressive ruins of L'Abbaye de Hambye and Mont Robin (276 metres), from where you have superb views of the countryside towards Suisse Normande (to the east), the spires of Coutances cathedral (to the north-west) and even the Channel Islands on a clear day. To the west, there is a zoo at Champrepus.

WHAT TO LOOK OUT FOR ...

Copper and pewter. Also cheese, foie gras, cider, pommeau and calvados.

WHERE TO GO FOR ...

COPPER
Atelier du Cuivre, 54 rue du Général-Huard, Villedieu. Tel: 33.51.31.85.

PEWTER
Maison d'Etain, 15 rue du Général-Huard, Villedieu-les-Poêles.
Tel: 33.51.05.08.

CHEESE
Société Fromagère Besnier Cécile, L'Acherie, Sainte-Cécile, nr Villedieu-les-Poêles. Tel: 33.50.83.44.

CIDER ETC.
Pierre Bourdon, La Janière, La Colombe, nr Villedieu-les-Poêles. Tel: 33.51.23.64.

FOIE GRAS
Véronique Brasy, Le Bourg, Fleury, nr Villedieu-les-Poêles. Tel: 33.50.01.88.

WHERE TO EAT ...

Le Moulin, D924, Champrepus, nr Villedieu-les-Poêles. Tel: 33.61.30.77.

Le Briseïs, D924, Beauchamps, nr Villedieu-les-Poêles. Tel: 33.61.34.74.

Les Gourmets, 10 place du Cardinal Grente, Percy, nr Villedieu-les-Poêles. Tel: 33.61.21.30.

WHERE TO EAT & STAY ...

Hôtel Saint-Pierre et Saint-Michel, 12 place de la République, Villedieu-les-Poêles. Tel: 33.61.00.11.

Le Fruitier, Place des Costils, Villedieu-les-Poêles. Tel: 33.90.51.00.

Manoir de l'Acherie, D554, Sainte-Cécile, nr Villedieu-les-Poêles. Tel: 33.51.13.87.

Hôtel Le Lion d'Argent, 73 rue de la Libération, La Haye-Pesnel, nr Villedieu-les-Poêles. Tel: 33.61.51.51.

Tessy-sur-Vire

WHAT TO LOOK OUT FOR ...

Calvados, pommeau and poiré. Also foie gras and dairy produce.

WHERE TO GO FOR ...

CALVADOS ETC.
Le Clos Minotte, Tessy-sur-Vire. Tel: 33.56.30.16.

FOIE GRAS
Elevage de la Rue, Fourneaux, nr Tessy-sur-Vire. Tel: 33.55.54.43.

DAIRY PRODUCE
D & P Desvages, GIE de la Poterie, Tessy-sur-Vire. Tel: 33.56.31.76.

Dominique Simon, Ferme de l'Isle, Moyon, nr Tessy-sur-Vire. Tel: 33.50.30.91.

S & R Viard, GAEC du Bourg Groux, Moyon, nr Tessy-sur-Vire. Tel: 33.55.73.67.

GAEC des Alpines, La Salmonière, Moyon, nr Tessy-sur-Vire. Tel: 33.56.32.42.

GAEC de la Balle, La Haye-Bellefonds, nr Tessy-sur-Vire. Tel: 33.61.20.44.

DEER
Lecharpentier, L'Asselotière, Saint-Vigor-des-Monts, nr Tessy-sur-Vire. Tel: 33.61.96.53.

WHERE TO EAT ...

Yves Fouchard, La Chapelle-sur-Vire, nr Tessy-sur-Vire. Tel: 33.56.32.83.

Les Bruyères, N175, Gouvets, nr Tessy-sur-Vire. Tel: 33.51.69.82.

WHERE TO EAT & STAY ...

Hôtel de France, Rue Saint-Pierre-et-Miquelon, Tessy-sur-Vire. Tel: 33.56.30.01.

Torigni-sur-Vire

This small town boasts a fine collection of tapestries, furniture and local sculpture in Le Château des Matignon, of which only the restored west wing still stands. Les Roches de Ham, to the west, stand 80 metres above the River Vire and provide a superb view of this delightful spot. A little further south you will find Château Angotière, of 15th century origin and in an idyllic wooded setting. Close by is the village of La Chapelle-sur-Vire, whose church has been a place of pilgrimage since the 12th century.

WHAT TO LOOK OUT FOR ...

Cider and foie gras.

WHERE TO GO FOR ...

CIDER
Cidrerie d'Elle & Vire, Condé-sur-Vire, nr Torigni-sur-Vire. Tel: 33.06.66.61.

FOIE GRAS
François Marie, La Brebissonnière, Saint-Symphorien-les-Buttes, nr Torigni-sur-Vire. Tel: 33.56.96.30.

WHERE TO EAT ...

Auberge de l'Alpado, 17 rue Havin, Torigni-sur-Vire. Tel: 33.55.09.90.

Auberge de l'Orangerie, 3 rue Victor-Hugo, Torigni-sur-Vire. Tel: 33.56.70.64.

WHERE TO EAT & STAY ...

Motel du Bocage, Les Landes, Giéville, nr Torigni-sur-Vire. Tel: 33.56.06.01.

D-Day Country

This tour takes in the famous coastline that – on 6 June 1944 – became the launching-pad from which the Allied troops eventually liberated France. The most convenient points for setting out are either Ouistreham or Cherbourg. Whether or not the D-Day landing sites – and countless monuments and museums – are of interest, this area to the east of Caen can also offer all of those specialities one would expect of the region – such as seafood and oysters, especially at Grandcamp-Maisy, the whole range of dairy produce centred round Isigny-sur-Mer, and an exceptional pottery centre at Noron-la-Poterie near Bayeux. And, of course, there is that famous tapestry in the town, and the fine cathedral.

YOUR ROUTE ...

D514 from Ouistreham to Courseulles-sur-Mer, Arromanches-les-Bains, Port-en-Bessin & Grandcamp-Maisy.

D514 then N13 to Isigny-sur-Mer.

(N13 from Cherbourg to Isigny-sur-Mer)

D5 to Le Molay-Littry & Bayeux.

D12 then D22 to Creully.

D141 to Colomby-sur-Thaon.

D79 to Caen.

See map overleaf.

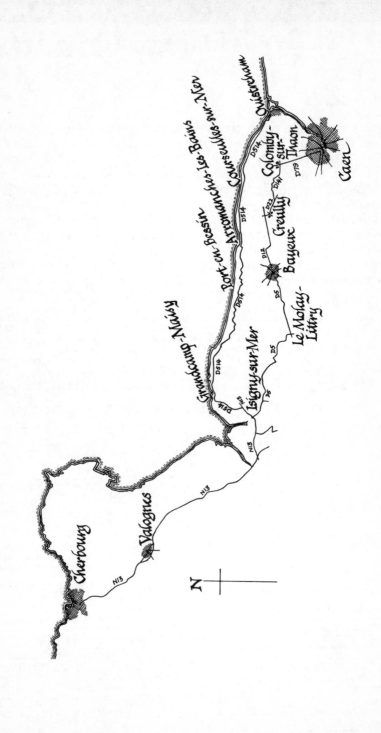

This popular resort, which has a large marina, is probably best known for its oysters. The beds all along the shore are used for maturing the crustacea. In June 1944, after the Juno Beach landings, the town welcomed a few famous faces – Winston Churchill, Charles de Gaulle and King George VI himself! You will find a remarkable display of sea-shells in La Maison de la Mer and can learn more about oyster culture at the walk-through – and walk in – aquarium. There is a good view from the nearby lighthouse at Ver-sur-Mer.

WHAT TO LOOK OUT FOR …

Oysters (renowned since Roman times), shellfish and crustacea. Also dairy produce.

WHERE TO GO FOR …

OYSTERS ETC.
J C Benoist, Parcs de l'Ile de Plaisance, Courseulles (dir. Arromanches).

La Chaumière, Courseulles (dir. Arromanches). Tel: 31.37.45.48.

DAIRY PRODUCE
Gilles Coiffier, Sainte-Croix-sur-Mer, nr Courseulles-sur-Mer. Tel: 31.22.23.62.

WHERE TO EAT …

La Pêcherie, Place du 6 Juin, Courseulles-sur-Mer. Tel: 31.37.45.84.

WHERE TO EAT & STAY …

Hôtel Le Gitan, Boulevard de la Plage, Courseulles-sur-Mer. Tel: 31.37.46.73.

Le Marsouin, 2 rue Charcot, Luc-sur-Mer, nr Courseulles-sur-Mer.
Tel: 31.97.32.08.

Grandcamp-Maisy

This is the main centre for the oysters of La Baie des Veys, considered among the most meaty and therefore ideal for cooking. More than 6,000 tonnes are harvested each year. Apart from the small fishing harbour, there is also a marina and, offshore, a collection of rocks. To the east, the 30-metre high limestone cliff, La Pointe du Hoc, overlooks Omaha Beach – scene of some of the most ferocious fighting during the D-Day operations – and offers superb views of the coastline around.

WHAT TO LOOK OUT FOR …

Oysters (particularly the *charnue*) and scallops. Also dairy produce and poultry.

WHERE TO GO FOR …

OYSTERS ETC.
André Taillepied, Base Conchylicole, Grandcamp-Maisy. Tel: 31.22.76.82.

Mme Aimard, La Noroise, Base Conchylicole, Grandcamp-Maisy.
Tel: 31.22.13.98.

Jean-Pierre Lasnon,
Base Conchylicole, Grandcamp-Maisy.
Tel: 31.22.19.13.

Guy Lecourtois, Base Conchylicole,
Grandcamp-Maisy. Tel: 31.22.76.57.

Guy Pourtier, Base Conchylicole,
Grandcamp-Maisy. Tel: 31.22.64.58.

Bernard Perron, Base Conchylicole,
Grandcamp-Maisy. Tel: 31.22.66.63.

Benoît Tronçon, Base Conchylicole,
Grandcamp-Maisy. Tel: 31.22.75.01.

DAIRY PRODUCE & POULTRY
Patrick Deshayes, opp Le Château,
Asnières-en-Bessin, nr Grandcamp-
Maisy. Tel: 31.22.44.12.

WHERE TO EAT ...

La Trinquette, Grandcamp-Maisy.
Tel: 31.22.64.90.

WHERE TO EAT & STAY ...

Hôtel de la Mer, 139 rue Aristide-
Briand, Grandcamp-Maisy.
Tel: 31.22.67.89.

Isigny-sur-Mer

For 300 years this town has been an important centre for Normandy's dairy industry, principally in the production of milk and butter. To the east, at La Cambe, is the imposing German Military Cemetery where 21,500 soldiers are buried, while the moated château at Colombières, whose imposing round towers dominate the adjoining marshland, is also worth a visit.

WHAT TO LOOK OUT FOR ...

Dairy produce (top grade classification in France) and toffees.

WHERE TO GO FOR ...

TOFFEES ETC.
Dupont d'Isigny, La Cambe, Isigny-
sur-Mer. Tel: 31.22.70.12.

CHEESE
Pierre Lanquetot d'Isigny,
La Blanche, Les Veys, nr Isigny-sur-Mer.
Tel: 31.22.00.55.

WHERE TO EAT ...

La Flambée, Isigny-sur-Mer.
Tel: 31.22.00.78.

Le Grand Café, 15 place du Général
de Gaulle, Isigny-sur-Mer.
Tel: 31.22.03.26.

La Rivière, Saint-Germain-du-Pert,
nr Isigny-sur-Mer. Must book.
Tel: 31.22.72.92.

WHERE TO EAT & STAY ...

Hôtel-Motel de France, 17 rue Emile
Demagny, Isigny-sur-Mer.
Tel: 31.22.00.33.

Aux Amis de la Route, N13,
Osmanville, nr Isigny-sur-Mer.
Tel: 31.22.14.84.

Bayeux

This charming town is dominated by the magnificent Norman-Gothic cathedral which mercifully, like much of its surroundings, survived the Allied Invasion of Normandy in June 1944. Much of the original architecture has been lovingly restored. The best-known treasure is, of course, the Bayeux Tapestry (La Tapisserie de la Reine Mathilde), housed in the Centre Guillaume le Conquérant. In 58 detailed scenes measuring a total of 70 metres it depicts those events of 1066 which led to William's victory over King Harold.

WHAT TO SEE ...

The Cathédrale Notre-Dame, with its crypt and the Chapter House, the Bayeux Tapestry, the 18th century Hôtel du Doyen housing the Bayeux lace workshop and Le Musée d'Art Sacré, Le Musée Baron Gérard, Le Jardin Botanique and the old town. In memory of the events of 1944, there are also Le Musée Mémorial de la Bataille de Normandie, Le Mémorial Charles de Gaulle and La Place Charles-de-Gaulle.

There is also much to see around Bayeux. To the south-west, you will discover the 12th century church at Saint-Loup-Hors, the pottery workshops lining the road through Noron-la-Poterie, Balleroy Château, L'Eglise Abbatiale (6th century origins) and the 13th century Bâtiments Conventuels at Cerisy-la-Forêt and the former mining centre at Le Molay-Littry with its Musée de la Mine. To the south lies L'Abbaye de Mondaye. To the east is château country, with castles at Crépon, Creully, Creullet, Lantheuil, Brécy and Vaussieux.

And, of course, Bayeux is one of the principal starting points for a tour of the D-Day beaches. To the north-east lies Arromanches-les-Bains, whose artificial harbour presents arguably one of the most impressive surviving memorials to the events of 1944. Just offshore there is a patchwork of massive metal structures, which have been left to commemorate this incredible piece of construction by the British invasion forces. Naturally enough, the town has its own Musée du Débarquement.

WHAT TO LOOK OUT FOR ...

Cider and goat's cheese. Also the pottery and other crafts. Special markets for foie gras at the start of July and in mid-December.

WHERE TO GO FOR ...

CIDER
Cidrerie Viard, Guéron, nr Bayeux. Tel: 31.92.09.15.

CHEESE
Le Bajocasse, Nonant, nr Bayeux. Tel: 31.92.05.38.

POTTERY
Poterie Dubost, Noyon-la-Poterie, nr Bayeux. Tel: 31.92.56.15.

Atelier Ceramique Turgis, Noyon-la-Poterie, nr Bayeux. Tel: 31.92.57.03.

Atelier du Chuquet, Le Molay-Littry, nr Bayeux. Tel: 31.22.18.76.

Hervé Coffignal, 2 rue du Calvaire, Trévières, nr Bayeux. Tel: 31.22.56.73.

STONE & MARBLE
SARL La Laiterie, Barbeville, nr Bayeux. Tel: 31.21.55.67.

Pascal Goujon, Les Feugrais, Nonant, nr Bayeux. Tel: 31.21.17.33.

LEATHER
Vaussieux, Vaux-sur-Seulles, nr Bayeux. Tel: 31.92.89.07.

La Piquenotière, Saint-Martin-de-Blagny, nr Bayeux. Must book.
Tel: 31.21.35.54.

Le Loucel, Colleville-sur-Mer, nr Bayeux. Must book. Tel: 31.22.40.95.

Le Manoir de la Drôme, 129 rue des Forges, Balleroy, nr Bayeux.
Tel: 31.21.60.94.

Le Lion d'Or (L), 71 rue Saint-Jean, Bayeux. Tel: 31.92.06.90.

Grand Hôtel du Luxembourg (M), 25 rue des Bouchers, Bayeux.
Tel: 31.92.00.04.

Château de Goville (L), D5, Le Breuil-en-Bessin, nr Bayeux. Tel: 31.22.19.28.

La Chenevière (L), Escures-Commes, nr Bayeux. Tel: 31.21.47.96.

Château d'Audrieu (L), Audrieu, nr Bayeux. Tel: 31.80.21.52.

Château de Sully (L), Route de Port-en-Bessin, Sully, nr Bayeux.
Tel: 31.22.29.48.

Ferme de la Rançonnière (M), Crépon, nr Bayeux. Tel: 31.22.21.73.

Hôtel Jeanne d'Arc (M), 2 rue de Bayeux, Tilly-sur-Seulles, nr Bayeux.
Tel: 31.80.80.13.

Hôtel Saint-Martin (M), 6 place Edmond-Paillaud, Creully, nr Bayeux.
Tel: 31.80.10.11.

Château du Baffy (M), Colombiers-sur-Seulles, Creully, nr Bayeux.
Tel: 31.08.04.57.

Château de Bellefontaine (L), 49 rue de Bellefontaine, Bayeux.
Tel: 31.22.00.10.

Hôtel d'Argouges (M), 21 rue Saint-Patrice, Bayeux. Tel: 31.92.88.86.

How to Get There ...

The ideal way to see Normandy, of course, is by car or coach. That means crossing The Channel by one of several ferry routes. The region boasts no less than four main passenger ports, with average crossing times varying from four to six hours – just over two by the new catamaran service from Newhaven to Dieppe. The regular daily services are supplied through Brittany Ferries, P&O and Stena Line. Needless to say, the prices are always competitive, so it is really a question of personal choice and convenience.

Incidentally, the Brighton to Fécamp 'passenger only' route has recently been resurrected. Anyone interested in this crossing is advised to check on the exact details.

The guide offers you a selection of tours to show the best of the many fascinating aspects of a region rich in history, culture and tradition. Each is based on one or more of the ferry ports, although it should be said that one can comfortably cross the region in a single day's drive. For a short stay – perhaps just a long weekend – you may wish to concentrate your visit on just one area and therefore your choice of crossing will be important.

Crossing The Channel

Newhaven–Dieppe
Stena Line provides four crossings per day in each direction by traditional ferry (all year) and the same by catamaran during the summer (three crossings each way off season).

Portsmouth–Le Havre
P&O provides an average of three crossings per day in each direction, although at certain times this is reduced to two.

Portsmouth–Caen (Ouistreham)
Brittany Ferries provides an average of three crossings per day in each direction, although at certain times this is reduced to two – and occasionally one.

Portsmouth–Cherbourg
P&O normally provides three crossings per day in each direction, although this is reduced to just one from the end of December till the middle of March.

Poole–Cherbourg
Brittany Ferries normally provides two crossing per day in each direction, although on certain days this is reduced to just one.

Southampton–Cherbourg
Stena Line provides an average of two crossings per day in each direction from the end of May till the middle of August – and a single crossing for most of the rest of the year.

For more Information

While you travel round Normandy, it may well be that you require more general – or specific – information than is contained in this guide. Remember that all main towns have their own tourist office where you can obtain details of the immediate area. These can be found under the title of Office de Tourisme or Syndicat d'Initiative.

Alternatively, you can contact the relevant *département* tourist office – Comité Départemental de Tourisme. Their addresses are as follows:

Calvados:
CDT
Place du Canada
14000 CAEN
Tel: 31.86.53.30.

Eure:
CDT
Hôtel du Département
Boulevard Georges-Chauvin
27000 EVREUX
Tel: 32.31.51.51.

Manche:
CDT
Maison du Département
50008 SAINT-LÔ Cedex
Tel: 33.05.98.70.

Orne:
CDT
88 rue Saint-Blaise
61001 ALENCON Cedex
Tel: 33.28.88.71.

Seine-Maritime:
CDT
6 rue Couronné
BP 60
76420 BIHOREL-LES-ROUEN
Tel: 35.59.26.26.